MEL BAY PRESENTS

GUITAR
Setup, Maintenance & Repair

by JOHN LEVAN

Cover Photo by David Johnson
Layout Design by Skip Anderson

1 2 3 4 5 6 7 8 9 0

Visit us on the Web at www.melbay.com — E-mail us at email@melbay.com

Foreword

Some years back, while walking through my factory, I was introduced to a young man by my then service manager at Taylor Guitars, Terry Myers. "Bob," he said, "this is John LeVan, the guy I've told you about who's got a repair shop going up in Auburn." "Auburn?" I thought, "What kind of business can a guy do in repairs up in Auburn?" Auburn is a little wooded town just north of Sacramento, California, and among my favorite spots, actually. The year was 1994 and John was determined to become one of our very first authorized service centers. Terry has since moved to other duties at Taylor Guitars, but at the time he was envisioning repairmen across the country that had the talent to work on our guitars the way we would; fast, efficient, and above all, able to diagnose the true problem with the guitar. Terry worked hard on that goal, but he needed raw talent and a good attitude from the applicants in order to accomplish the task. So here was John LeVan, spending his time in our repair shop learning our guitars, our methods, our diagnosing procedures; he was learning to have our eyes.

Well, he went home to Auburn, and it came to pass that he grew tremendously in knowledge and eventually relocated to Nashville. This was music to our ears because we now had a man in place in Music City, USA to take care of the many, many Taylor owners there. Nashville is the place with probably the highest population of professionals who use our guitars. John established himself there as an expert guitar repairman who could give great service to people who needed it, both the players and us at Taylor. Our relationship with John has been a joy.

We all know the idea of any category being divided into good, better, and best. I see a lot of people who want to do guitar repairs and be an expert at it. But I don't see people who are hungry for knowledge and experience on how to really be an expert, and are willing to put in the time necessary and check their ego at the door in order to learn. This expertise I'm referring to starts with the skill of looking at a guitar and deciding what the problem is. (You have no idea how many times a neck is refretted when what the guitar actually needs is to be humidified!) After that, it moves on to the expertise of how to effectively accomplish the repair, all in the given time allotted, and then returning that guitar to its owner at the promised time. John LeVan has done more than gather knowledge, he has amassed it. When I read this book I see John's habits on the page - look at the guitar, assess the problem, clean the workbench and gather the right tools, wash your hands, put on a smile, and get it done properly with the least effort. It's amazing that after less than a lifetime of guitar repair John can be so organized and energized to put it all in the form of a book like this, thus, passing on the information to others. Please take a good look and learn some things from a person who is an expert learner himself.

Bob Taylor

Dedication

I dedicate this book to my wife, Wendy and my daughters, Sarah and Sophia who every day remind me that life is precious, fragile and miraculous.

Acknowledgments

I would like to thank all of the people who have encouraged, supported and apprenticed me in the craft of luthrie. Special thanks to my Lord Jesus Christ for creating me and giving me a wife that will tolerate me. To my wife, Wendy, for putting up with me for all of these years. Lt. Col. John Nargoso Bilson, for making a man out of me. Brad Shreve, from Larry's Music Center in Wooster, Ohio, the first person to teach me anything about guitar repair. Karl (with a 'K') Mischler, for teaching me how to play the guitar. Michael Lewis, for including me in the creation of the Sacramento Valley Luthiers Guild. Bob Taylor and Terry Myers, for believing in me enough to let me study at the Taylor® Guitar Factory and showing me how a real repair shop is run, and for the great photographs and diagrams. Tom Anderson®, for affording me the opportunity to learn an excellent technique of fretwork, and opening my eyes to a new temperament. Everyone at Gruhn® Guitars, for all of their support and friendship, especially Ben Burgett, Andy Jellison, and Dave Lautner for teaching me cutting-edge repair techniques. Seymour Duncan ®, thanks for all the great diagrams, support and products. Lloyd Baggs from L.R. Baggs®, for the excellent pictures, product and information for the book. Jay Hostetler from Stewart-MacDonald®, for providing such great tools. Skip Anderson, for great photos and invaluable advice. Finally, to all of the good people who have trusted me with their instruments - without all of you, I'd probably still be working in a gas station.

Guitar Care, Setup & Repair

Guitar Repair and Maintenance Kit

It's important to use the correct tool for the job. Likewise it is important to buy quality tools that will last. The quality of your tools is reflected in your work, and your work is your calling card. Every guitar you work on is like a résumé, so be sure to do your best. Below is a list of tools and materials recommended to perform the tasks outlined in this book. Here is what you need to get started:
The six-piece screwdriver set should include small, medium and large-tip Phillips screwdrivers, and small, medium and large-tip flathead screwdrivers. These tools are used to adjust intonation and install and remove neck bolts, pickguard screws, pickups, etc.

6-Piece Screwdriver Set
6-Piece Miniature Needle File Set
Precision Scale (Rule)
14-Piece Hex Key Set
10-Piece Nut File Set
String Winder
Cordless Drill
Wire Cutters
Polish Cloth
Fret Files (half-round)
Fret Leveling Bar
Straightedges
Fretting Hammer
Large Flush-Cut Dykes
Small Flush-Cut Dykes

Fret Bending Tool
Bag of Buckshot
Hemostats
Alligator Clips
Vacuum (with brush attachment)
Toothbrush
Soldering Iron
Nut Drivers
X-Acto® Knives
Magnifying Lamp
Drill and Bits
Guitar Tuner
Humidifier
Safety Glasses
Mechanical Pencil

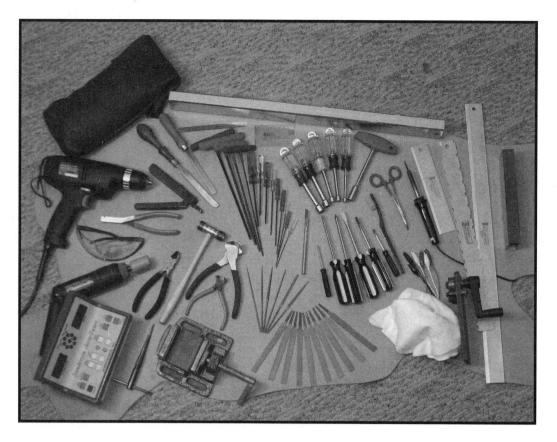

FIGURE 1.1 Here are the tools you will need to complete the projects in this book. (Photo by Skip Anderson)

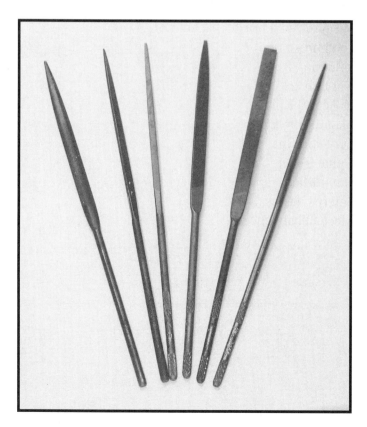

FIGURE 1.2 The six-piece miniature needle file set should be single-cut, Swiss, and made of carbide steel. (Photo by John LeVan)

This set should include:

1. Round File
2. Flat File
3. Square File
4. Half-Round File
5. Three-Cornered File
6. Flat Triangular File

These files are used to carve and intonate a bridge saddle, file fret ends, spot level a fret, clean out the slot for a string nut, cut slots into a string nut, file the bridge pin holes, etc.

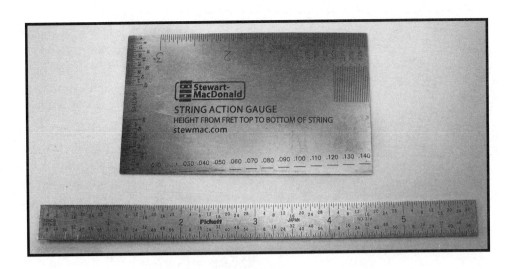

FIGURE 1.3A,B The precision scale rule is a small, six-inch, metal ruler that measures from 1/64" on up. This is important because many of the measurements in this book are in 1/64" and 1/32". Be sure that your scale has good contrast to make it easier to read. 1.3 B, An Action Gauge® (sold by Stewart-MacDonald®) is an excellent tool for measuring the action on a guitar. (Photos by John LeVan)

An important element of your tool collection is a 14-piece hex key set. This set will be used for adjusting, bridge saddles, trussrods, some pickup pole pieces, access panels, etc. I recommend the following sizes; .05", 1/16", 3/32", 1/8", 5/32", 9/64", 3/16", 1mm, 1.5mm, 2mm, 2.5mm, 3mm, 4mm, 5mm.

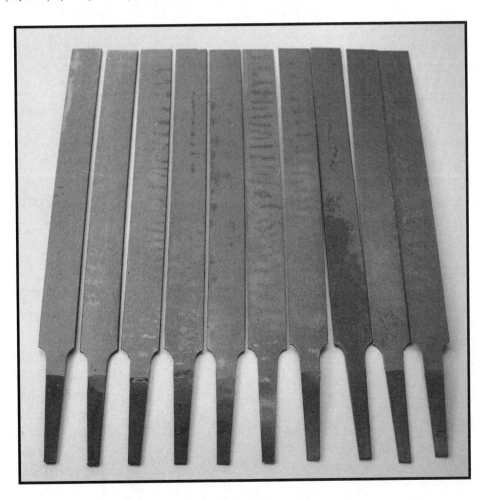

FIGURE 1.4 The 10-piece nut file set is critical to carving a string nut as well as the final steps to a setup. You'll need these sizes; .010, .012, .016, .022, .026, .032, .036, .040, .046, .052. The above listed files are two-sided, made of carbide steel and are absolutely necessary. (Photo by John LeVan)

FIGURE 1.5 There are many types of string winders on the market. Varying from 99¢ to $29, this is one tool that will save you a lot of time and energy. I prefer the type that fits into a cordless drill, thus speeding up the restringing process and minimizing fatigue and the risk of developing tendonitis. (Photo by John LeVan)

When choosing a cordless drill, I recommend a rechargeable model with a pistol grip, torque clutch, reverse capability, and at least 600 rpm. As for wire cutters, a six-inch pair of angled pliers works well. The only polish cloth I use in my shop is a 100-percent cotton, birdseye-weave cloth diaper.

FIGURE 1.6 Fret files are available in many sizes as well as grades of coarseness. I recommend keeping a small, medium and large two-sided fret file in fine and coarse cut. Carbide steel and diamond-coated are two of the most common fret file types available. The differences will be discussed in Chapter 8. (Photo by Skip Anderson)

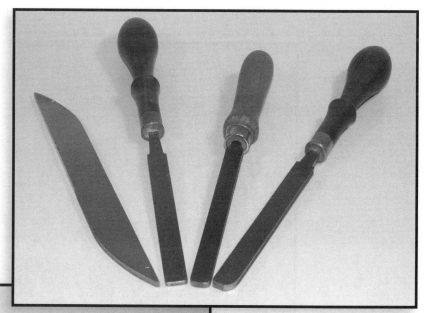

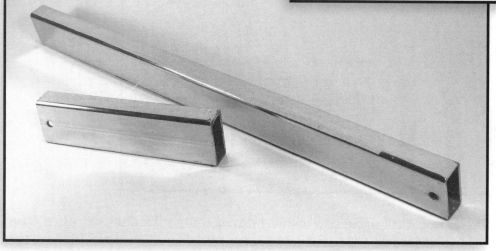

FIGURE 1.7 Fret leveling bars are made of finely milled, chrome plated bar stock and come in several sizes. The 24" and 8" leveling bars get the most use around my shop. Using self-adhesive sandpaper, the 24" is great for leveling frets, fretboards and burnishing. The 8" leveling bar is perfect for spot leveling. (Photo by Skip Anderson)

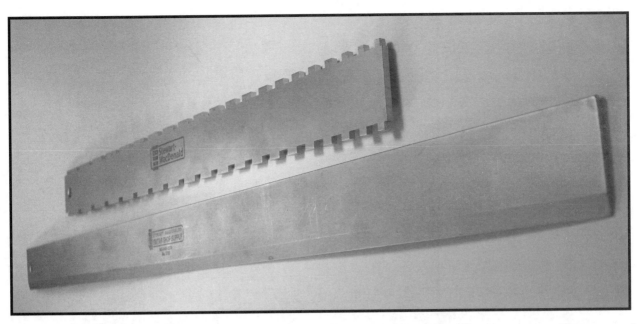

FIGURE 1.8 Straightedges are essential for sighting a neck and checking the frets to see if they are level. There are several sizes and types that I recommend starting from 1", 4", 6", 12", 24" to 36" and even one that is notched out where the frets are to check that the fretboard is "true" (straight with the proper radius). (Photo by Skip Anderson)

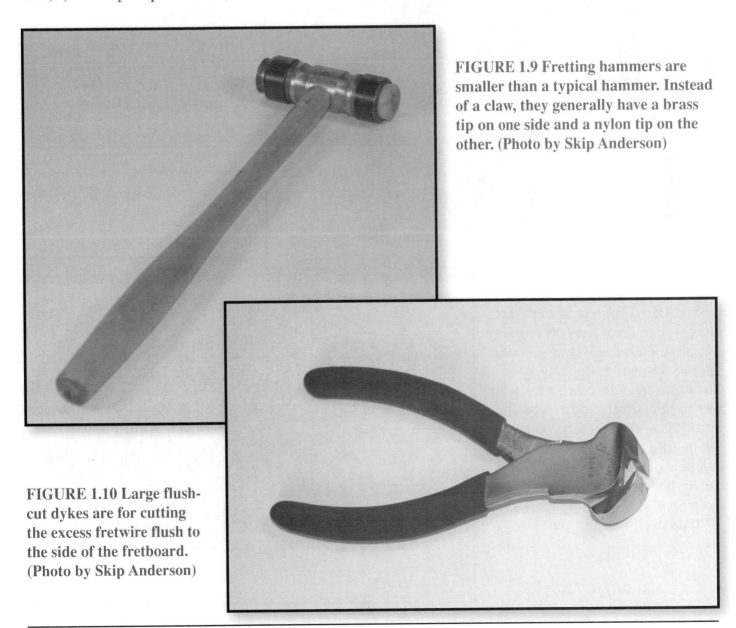

FIGURE 1.9 Fretting hammers are smaller than a typical hammer. Instead of a claw, they generally have a brass tip on one side and a nylon tip on the other. (Photo by Skip Anderson)

FIGURE 1.10 Large flush-cut dykes are for cutting the excess fretwire flush to the side of the fretboard. (Photo by Skip Anderson)

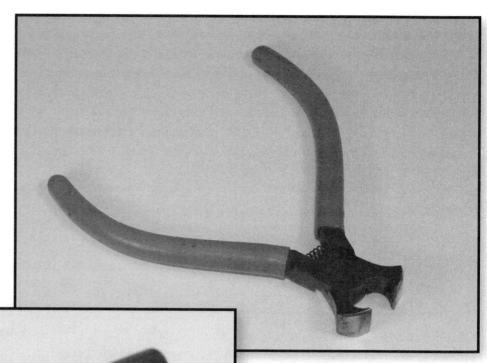

FIGURE 1.11 Small flush-cut dykes are used to remove frets from the fretboard.
(Photo by Skip Anderson)

FIGURE 1.12 A fret-bending tool is used for bending the fretwire to the radius of the fretboard.
(Photo by Skip Anderson)

FIGURE 1.13 A bag of buckshot has several great uses other than running off an unwelcome guest. I use a 25-pound bag of no. 6 shot wrapped in leather as a neck rest when doing fretwork, setups and carving a string nut. Wrapping it in leather and then sealing it closed will help to prevent potentially harmful lead dust from escaping.
(Photo by Skip Anderson)

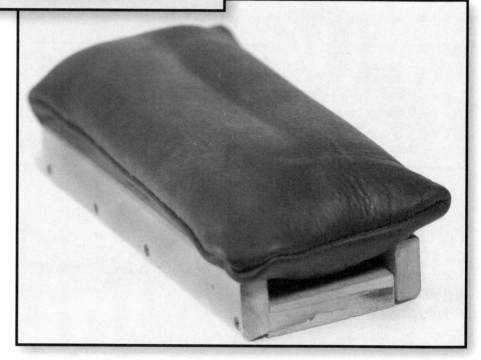

Hemostats are great for preventing fingertip burns when soldering. They are also great for do-it-yourself surgeries. Alligator clips are helpful when tracing wires and experimenting with different wiring combinations.

FIGURE 1.14 A vacuum with a round brush attachment will help you clean up metal filings and dust when working on a guitar. While I prefer a small shop vac, most uprights have all the attachments you'll need – just don't tell your spouse I said to use it. (Photo by Skip Anderson)

A medium to hard bristle toothbrush is perfect for scrubbing while applying lemon oil to your fretboard. Remember – it's not nice to use someone else's toothbrush without asking first!

FIGURE 1.15 Soldering irons come in many sizes and wattages. A 35 to 45 watt soldering iron is as hot as you'll need. If you have one with a reversible tip, I offer a simple modification that will speed up fret removal in Chapter 8. (Photo by Skip Anderson)

There are nine nut driver sizes that will be the most useful. 1/4", 5/16", 9/32", 11/32", 7/16", 1/2", 9/16", 6mm and 10mm are used for everything from adjusting a trussrod to tightening an endpin jack. X-Acto® knife sets are very handy around the shop. They come with several types of replacement blades and handles. These are used for scoring, cleaning glue out of a fret slot, etc. Magnifying lamps help you see detail that you normally can't see with the naked eye. Warning – viewing your work through a lens can be a very humbling experience. An electric drill and bits are needed when boring out the endblock to install an endpin jack, installing an acoustic guitar pickup and all those other projects that require more torque than what your cordless drill has. You will need bits in all standard (not metric) sizes from 1/16" to 1/8". You may also want a tapered ream for boring to install an endpin jack.

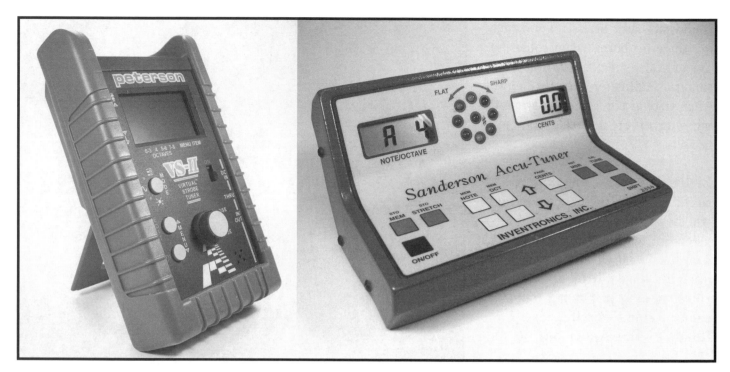

FIGURE 1.16 There are so many choices when it comes to choosing a guitar tuner. Most tuners are really not accurate enough to intonate a guitar properly. My shop tuner is accurate to +\- 1/100 of one cent. One whole tone = 100 cent. Most tuners are accurate to +/- three to five cent. I recommend a tuner that is at least +/- one cent for intonating a guitar. Most guitar tuners publish their accuracy ratings in their brochures. (Photo by John LeVan)

FIGURE 1.17 Humidifiers are one of the least expensive ways to prevent damage to a guitar. Our shop has warm mist humidifiers in each room; there are also humidifiers you install inside your guitar for transporting and storage. Humidifiers will be covered in detail in Chapter 2. (Photo by John LeVan)

Materials: Here is a list of the most common materials needed for general guitar repair and maintenance.

- Wood Glue (Tightbond® I and Tightbond® II, RBC® Epoxy)
- 1,500 Grit Self-Adhesive Sandpaper
- 220 Grit Self-Adhesive Sandpaper
- Super Glue®, Thick and Thin
- Super Glue® Accelerator
- Super Glue® Solvent
- Electronics Cleaner
- Rosin Core Solder
- 0000 Steel Wool
- Compressed Air
- Masking Tape
- Guitar Polish
- Razor Blades
- Suction Cup
- Lemon Oil
- Q-Tips®
- Wire

FIGURE 1.18 Here are the materials and supplies needed to complete the repairs in this book. (Photo by Skip Anderson)

Wood glue is needed for structural repairs. Tightbond® I is great for neck resets and bridge plate repairs. Tightbond® II is better for broken headstocks, body cracks and bridge reglues. RBC® Epoxy is good for crack repairs that require color matching. It can be mixed with fresco powder to match the paint or lacquer color of the guitar you are repairing. Super Glue® (cyanoacrylite) is manufactured by several companies. Zap® and Jet® are two that have given me great results. They come in a wide range of viscosities, from water thin to the thickness of molasses. I use the ultra thin, thin and thick the most. This type of glue works great for securing a string nut, loose frets and minor touch-ups on acrylic and polyurethane finishes. Be sure to also have Super Glue® accelerator (to speed up drying time) and Super Glue® solvent (in case you glue your finger to your chin; Pennington doctrine). Self-adhesive sandpaper is a must for any repair shop. The 1500-grit paper is best for polishing (burnishing) frets and polishing bone string nuts and saddles. It also comes in handy to sand out finish scratches. Use 220-grit sandpaper for fret leveling and carving string nuts and bridge saddles. When choosing an electronics cleaner, chose one that is safe for all plastics. Some types of cleaner can damage the plastic parts in switches and potentiometers. The only type of solder you'll need for a guitar is rosin core solder. Do not use acid core solder on the electronics of a guitar unless your goal is to destroy its electronics. 0000 grade Steel wool is needed to do a final polish on the frets as well as to clean the fretboard. Never use anything more coarse on a guitar; it could damage the frets. Compressed air is used to remove dust from electronic components. Low-tack 3" masking tape will be useful to tape off pickups while cleaning. Most guitar polishes will work fine on a variety of finishes, just don't use any polish on satin finishes or it will make them look inconsistent and hazy. Razor blades are used to scrape fretboards, binding and miscellaneous tasks. A small suction cup is ideal for removing stubborn control panels. Lemon oil is the best substance to condition a rosewood or ebony fretboard. It is highly recommended to condition and clean your guitar each time you restring. Q-Tips® are an absolute necessity whenever you use glue of any type. They are also handy for cleaning hard to reach places like under a bridge saddle or between your toes. 16-gauge cloth-wrapped wire is my wire of choice. There are several brands available and most are adequate. Below is a list of sources for purchasing the tools and materials listed in this book.

- LeVan's Guitar Services (615) 251-8884
  www.guitarservices.com

- Luthiers Mercantile International® (800) 477-4437
  www.LMII.com

- Stewart-MacDonald® (800) 848-2273
  www.stewmac.com

- All Parts® (800) 327-8942
  www.allparts.com

- Allied Lutherie LTD. (707) 431-3760
  www.alliedlutherie.com

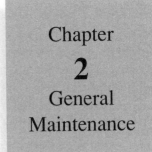
Hygiene

One of the most overlooked aspects of owning a guitar is cleaning and conditioning it regularly. Why is this so important? Because the more you play your guitar the more dirt, sweat and oils build up on it. As a result, your strings, frets and bridge receive the brunt of the damage. The acid in sweat and the oils from your fingers corrode the strings causing them to lose their bright tone. Likewise sweat and oils condense on the frets causing the wood around them to deteriorate. If left unconditioned, the fretboard and bridge can and will crack.

The key to preventing corrosion, cracking and poor guitar hygiene is to clean and condition your guitar every time you change your strings.

So how do you prevent these filthy afflictions from ravaging your guitar? It all starts with good hygiene.

The first step to good guitar hygiene is player cleanliness

- Wash your hands before you play
- Wipe your strings with a clean dry cloth after playing
- Make your friends wash their hands before you let them play your guitar

Good hygiene is good guitar care!

It also helps to store your guitar in its case and occasionally vacuum your case.

Materials needed

- 0000 Steel Wool (only 0000, never anything coarser)
- Vacuum (with brush attachment)
- Toothbrush
- Paper Towels
- Masking Tape (only for maple or blond fretboard, and/or to cover the pickups on an electric guitar)
- Lemon Oil
- Guitar Polish

Cleaning

There are a few fundamental steps to cleaning your guitar. The first step is to remove the strings – YES ALL OF THEM. It does not damage the guitar to remove all the strings at one time. Next, you need to scrub the fretboard with 0000 steel wool in the direction of the grain of the wood. This will clean the dirt and grime off of your fretboard as well as polish the frets. DO NOT USE 0, 00 or 000 steel wool, <u>only 0000</u>. If your guitar has a maple or blonde fretboard, then you'll need to either cover the wood with masking tape (only exposing the metal frets) or skip using the steel wool. 0000 Steel wool is a fine grit steel wool that won't damage the frets or fretboard. Avoid getting it into the electronics or on the finish.

If you are cleaning an electric guitar, be sure to cover the pickups with masking tape to prevent the steel wool from attaching to the pickup coils. The pickup coils are magnetic and will attract the steel wool. A low-tack, 3" or 4" masking tape is recommended for taping off the pickups. Cover them completely to prevent the steel wool from collecting around the pickup. Steel wool can cause the pickup to become microphonic and feedback.

Scrubbing the Fretboard

Scrubbing the fretboard will remove dirt, dead skin cells and other things that collect on your fretboard. You should do this every time you change your strings. The steps are as follows:

• Scrub the frets using the 0000 steel wool "with the grain" of the wood. Ninety-nine percent of the time "with the grain" means parallel to the length of the neck.

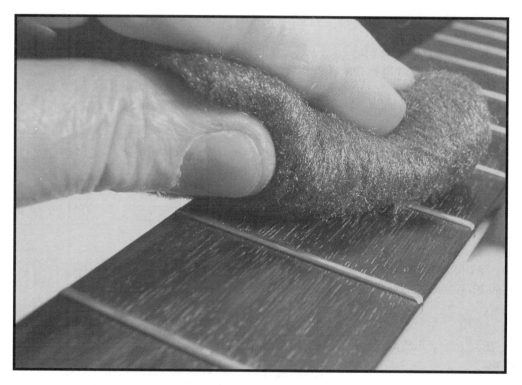

FIGURE 2.1 Scrub the fretboard with the grain, not against the grain. (Photo by John LeVan)

• After the fretboard is clean and the frets are polished, use a vacuum to remove all of the steel wool from the guitar. Make sure you vacuum the entire guitar and around the bench too. Remove masking tape.

Conditioning

Conditioning your guitar is easy. All you need is a toothbrush, lemon oil and paper towels.

•　　　Just dip your toothbrush into the lemon oil and then scrub the fretboard. Make sure that you cover all of the fretboard. The great thing about lemon oil is that you can't over oil your fretboard, it will only absorb what it needs.

•　　　After the lemon oil settles into the wood for a few minutes, simply wipe off the excess with a dry paper towel.

FIGURE 2.2 Most toothbrushes won't damage the fretboard. Don't be afraid of scrubbing it into the wood. (Photo by John LeVan)

Now is a good time to clean the rest of the body using a damp paper towel and a few drops of lemon oil. This process will make your guitar look and perform at its best.

Restringing

After thoroughly cleaning and conditioning your guitar, you are ready to restring it. Depending upon what kind of guitar you have (classical, electric, acoustic, bass, etc.) there are several techniques that can be applied. For a classical guitar or nylon-string guitar, the strings are tied on using a looping method. There is a standard method for restringing an acoustic guitar or bass. For an electric, it can be complex or very simple, depending on the instrument's hardware.

Tools Needed
•   String Winder (manual or electric)
•   String Cutters (end cutters, dykes, nippers)
•   Guitar Tuner
•   Patience

FIGURE 2.3 Electric or manual, a good string winder is essential to restringing a guitar. Likewise, a 6" pair of end cutters and an accurate guitar tuner are a must. (Photo by John LeVan)

Note: Classical or nylon-string guitars are the most challenging to restring.

When Restringing a Classical Guitar
Make sure that you do not over wind the strings (i.e. wrap the string too many times around the post). This can cause a world of tuning problems. Likewise, under winding the string is just as bad. Tie the strings using a looping method. Notice that the two treble strings, (B and E) are each looped through the bridge twice. This technique will minimize all the extra stretching that the string will incur. Classical strings stretch for several days before they settle into tune. It's also a good idea to singe the ends of the treble strings with a lighter before you tie them on. This prevents any additional string slippage.
See Figure 2.4 A-D on the next page

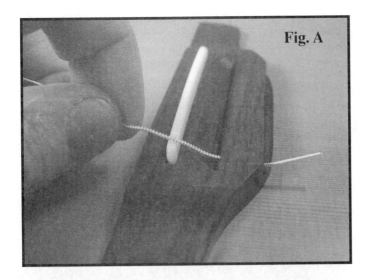

Fig. A

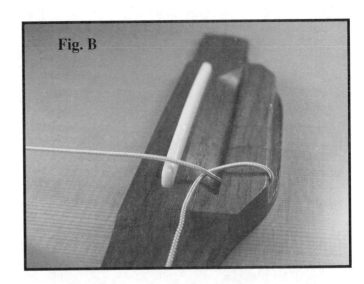

Fig. B

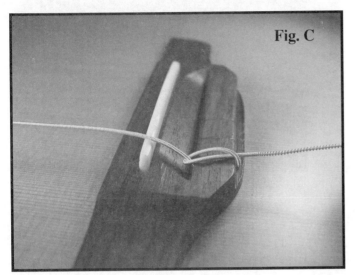

Fig. C

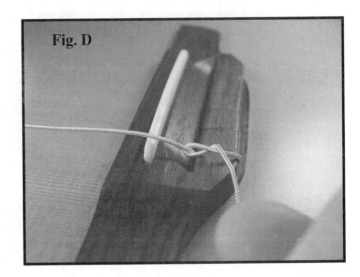

Fig. D

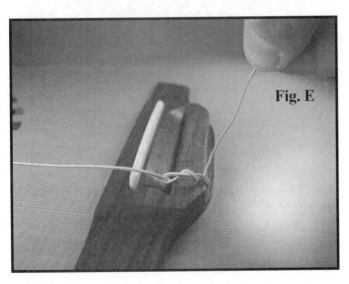

Fig. E

FIGURE 2.4A - D pull the string through the bridge, then over the top of the bridge, under and around itself (counterclockwise), then wrap the string under itself, with the final wrap on the backside of the bridge. (Photos by John LeVan)

Next, tie the strings onto the tuning key roller. This is where it gets a little more complex. But don't worry, you'll catch on once you've done a few more restrings. Note that the two E-string windings are wound in opposite directions, and the rest of the strings are wound towards each other. This is part of the headstock design. Stretch! Slowly stretch the strings by gently gripping the string with your thumb, index and middle fingers and then slowly pull the string while gliding your fingers along the length of the string. Be careful not to pull too hard, the string might break. If you glide too fast, you could burn your fingers! After you stretch the strings, tune, tune and retune.

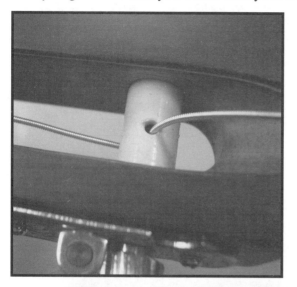

Fig. A

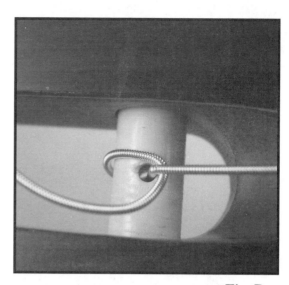

Fig. B

Fig. C

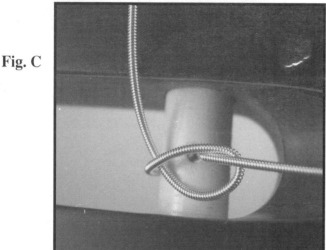

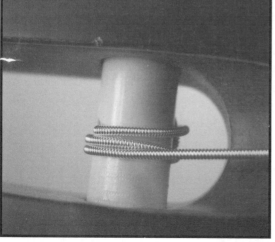

Fig. E

Fig. D

FIGURE 2.5A - E, Pull the string through the tuning key peg, then around the back of the peg, under and around itself (clockwise); then, wrap the string under itself and give two firm tugs. (Gardner Doctrine) (Photos by John LeVan)

When Stringing a Steel-String Acoustic

Gently curl the ball end of the string before you insert it into the bridge pin hole. Then push in the bridge pin and gently pull up on the string. This will lock the string into place and prevent the bridge pin from flying across the room. Next you need to tie the string to the tuning key post (See Figure 2.7). Always wind the string from the inside of the tuning key peg, never from the outside.* It is important not to overwrap nor underwrap the strings. Never wrap a string over itself, this can cause tuning problems and string breakage (See Figure 2.8). For the best results, use three to four wraps around the post. Slowly stretch the strings by gently gripping the string with your thumb, index and middle fingers and then slowly pull the string while gliding your fingers along the length of the string. Be careful not to pull too hard, the string might break. If you glide too fast, you could burn your fingers! Always gently stretch the strings and tune, tune and retune. After being properly stretched, the strings may drift out of tune periodically, but not by an extreme amount.

FIGURE 2.6 Gently curl the ball end of the string, but be careful not to bend it too far and break it. Curling the string will help it to lock onto the bridge plate, thus diminishing any string slippage at the bridge. (Photo by John LeVan)

* Winding the strings beginning on the inside of the peg will reduce string breakage. Over wrapping and under wrapping the strings will cause slippage resulting in tuning problems.

FIGURE 2.7 When you restring a steel-string guitar, always start from the inside of the tuning key peg, not the outside. The tuning keys are designed to tighten the strings when you turn them counter-clockwise. (Photo by John LeVan)

FIGURE 2.8 Wrapping the string over itself can cause string breakage and tuning problems. For the best results, wrap the string around the tuning key post in a downward direction using three or four wraps per string. (Photo by John LeVan)

The bridge assembly includes

- Bridge
- Bridge Pins
- Bridge Saddle
- Bridge Plate
- Strings

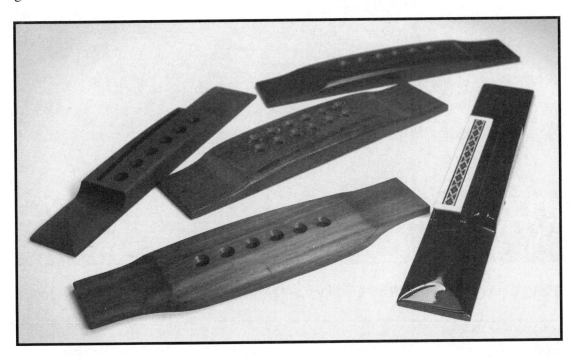

FIGURE 2.9 Acoustic guitar bridges are made from ebony, ivory, rosewood, Micarta® and even plastic. Bridge pins help to push the ball end of the strings into the bridge plate (pin plate), which is usually made from either maple or rosewood. The bridge saddle can be made from plastic, bone, ivory, graphite, brass, Micarta® or wood. Bone and ivory tend to give the most volume and dynamic range. Plastic and graphite have the least amount of volume and dynamic range. (Photo by John LeVan)

Note: Acoustic guitars are among the easiest to restring. However, watch out for flying bridge pins!

When Restringing an Electric Guitar.

Most electric guitars like the Strat®, Tele® and Les Paul®-style guitars are pretty basic. You just run the string through either the tailpiece or the bridge and then tie the strings onto the tuning key post. Some electric guitars have a locking tremolo system. Locking tremolo systems require hex keys to lock and unlock the string in order to do a restring. Like the acoustic guitar, you only want between three and four wraps around the post. Too few wraps will result in the string slipping out of tune, too many will result in the string stretching out of tune. There are a few techniques that may be helpful to you in order to get a uniform wrap for each string.

FIGURE 2.10 A tailpiece holds the strings in place as they lie over the bridge. (Photo by John LeVan)

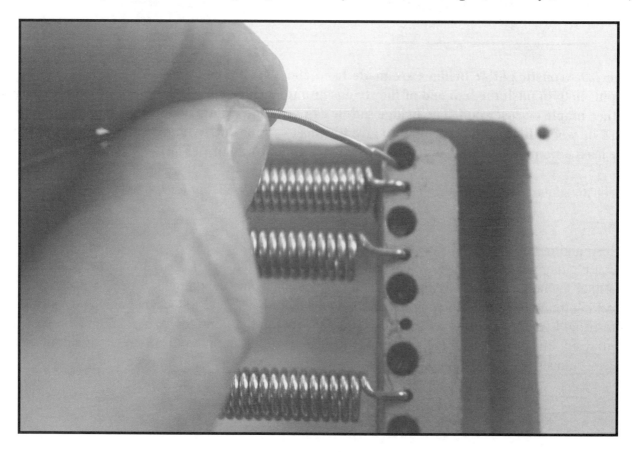

FIGURE 2.11 Tremolo-style bridges are strung from behind through the inertia or tailblock.
(Photo by John LeVan)

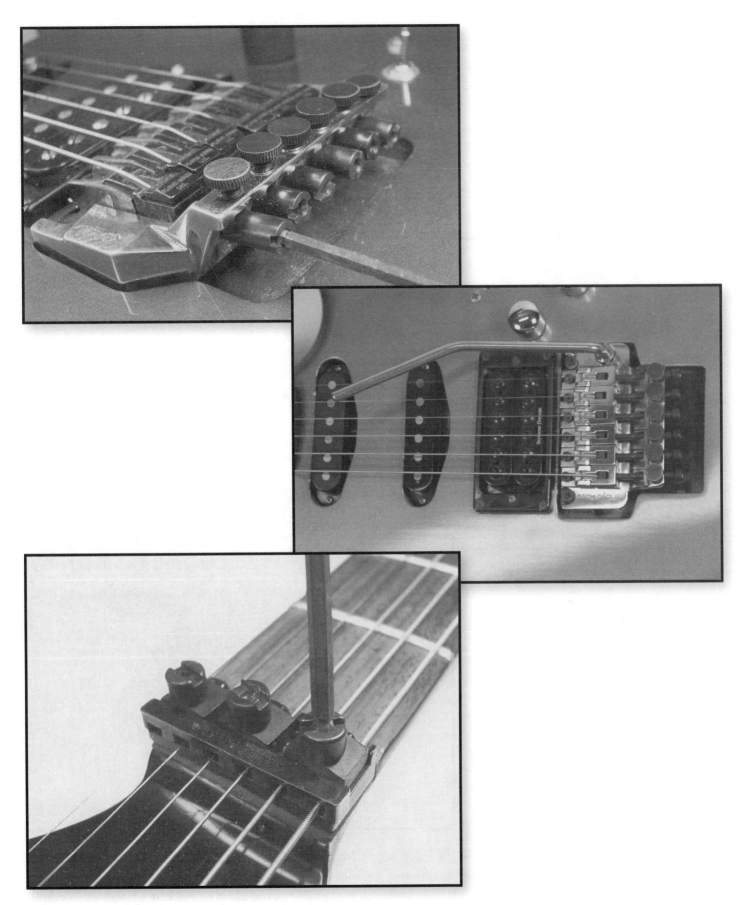

FIGURE 2.12A,B,C, Locking tremolos require hex keys to lock and unlock the strings from the bridge saddles and at the locking string nut. (Photos A and C by John LeVan) (Photo 2.12B by Skip Anderson)

The bridge assembly includes

- Intonation Screws
- Saddle Height Adjustment Screws
- Inertia Block
- Bridge Saddle
- Bridge Plate
- Tremolo Arm
- Spring Claw
- Tremolo Springs

FIGURE 2.13 A-B The intonation screws are for adjusting (you guessed it) intonation. The saddle height adjustment screws adjust the saddles up and down. The inertia block holds the ball end of the strings and acts as a counterbalance in tandem with the tremolo springs. The spring claw is used to adjust the tremolo flush to the body of the guitar. The bridge plate connects all the other components together.
(Photos by John LeVan)

Measure using the posts

To achive the correct number of string wraps on the tuning key post (of a guitar with all six keys on one side of the headstock), just pull the string three or four posts past the one you are going to wrap the string. Then, mark the string by bending it where it meets that third or fourth post; the bend will show you where the string should end when you pull it through the intended post. For example, when installing the low E string, pull it to the D or G string post and

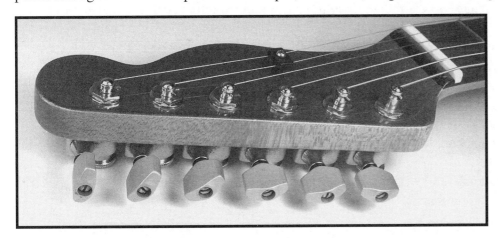

bend it where it lines up with that post. Then run it through the low E post up to the bend in the string and begin to wind the string onto the post. Always wind the string downward on the post, never upward or over itself. Wrapping the string over itself can cause string breakage and tuning problems. Finally, tune the guitar using an accurate guitar tuner (see Figure 1.16).

FIGURE 2.14 This guitar has all six tuning keys on one side of the headstock. This is also referred to as "six-in-line." (Photo by John LeVan)

FIGURE 2.15 Bend the string after pulling it three or four posts beyond the one being tied. This is an easy and accurate way to mark the end of the string before you start winding it onto the appropriate tuning key post.
(Photo by John LeVan)

FIGURE 2.16 Always wind the string downward, never upward or over itself. The goal is to create three to four tight wraps around the tuning key post. (Photo by John LeVan)

Transporting and Storage

When transporting and storing your guitar it's important to do so in a consistent environment. When shipping a guitar:

- Slightly detune the strings just in case it is jarred while in transit. A sudden impact can cause structural damage when the guitar is under tension.
- Install a fretguard to prevent the strings from damaging the frets if the guitar is dropped or jarred. A piece of cardboard or file folder will work.
- Secure your guitar in a quality ATA-certified guitar case and be sure that it doesn't have any wiggle room. *A snug case makes for a safer guitar.*
- Place all peripheral equipment in either the storage compartment of the case or in a separate bag. Do not leave anything in the case that can slide, fall or bounce on or into your guitar.

Detuning the strings (a few turns on each key) will help prevent undue tension on the guitar.
This is especially important for acoustic guitars.

FIGURE 2.17 Fretguards will prevent any damage to your frets from an impact on the guitar case. The fretguard slides between the frets and the strings, protecting the frets from the strings cutting into them during an impact. (Photo by John LeVan)

ATA® certified cases are approved for air travel. They are generally made from plywood, metal or ABS® plastic. Even with an ATA® certified case, it is important that the guitar does not move freely within the case. If the case fits loosely, I recommend using a towel or foam rubber to secure the guitar within the case.

Always store peripheral items such as a tuner, capo and string cutters, etc. in the middle compartment of the case. No good can come of a pair of string cutters bouncing off your guitar while in transit.

If you must store your guitar for any length of time, it needs to be in a consistent environment. That means the temperature and humidity should not fluctuate much more than 10 degrees and 10 percent respectively. 70 to 80° Fahrenheit is relatively safe, and 40 - 50% humidity is best. Again, it's a good idea to detune your guitar a whole step down (from standard pitch) for a long period of storage.

Humidity and Temperature

Humidity is the amount of moisture in the air. Too much or too little humidity can make your guitar sound, play and look very bad, 40 to 50% is the ideal amount of humidity for a guitar. If a guitar is left in an environment that is too hot or too cold (like the trunk of a car on a hot day), the result can be devastating. It only takes a few hours of heat to melt the glue that holds your guitar together. Acoustic instruments are affected more often than electric guitars because they are made from thinner pieces of wood and are under more stress and tension. All instruments, however, need a consistent environment. Here is a list of problems that occur as a result of extremely low humidity:

- Structural Cracks (bridge, neck, top, back, sides)
- Sharp Fret Ends (caused by the fretboard shrinking)
- Warped Neck
- Loose Braces
- Glue Failure
- Cracked Finish (finish checking)
- String Rattle
- Intonation and Tuning Problems

FIGURE 2.18 This guitar was badly damaged by low humidity. Notice the sunken top, excessively fore-bowed neck, and the high neck angle. There is usually extreme internal damage that requires extensive repair. (Illustration provided by the Taylor Guitar® Company)

How to Gauge Humidity

There are several products on the market to help you identify the humidity level in your environment. I recommend a digital gauge that measures both temperature and humidity. Most hardware stores as well as home improvement stores stock them; they retail from $14 to $30. Regardless of which one you choose, consider it to be a very cheap insurance policy for your guitar.

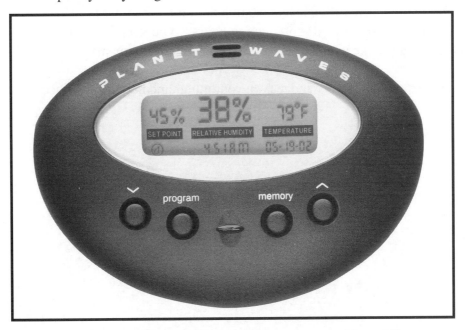

FIGURE 2.19 Most hygrometers will show both the temperature and humidity. (Photo provided by J. D'Addario & Co®.)

How to Control Humidity

I recommend two types of humidifiers depending upon where and how your guitar is stored. If your guitar is outside of its case, then I recommend a warm-mist room humidifier. Used with your hygrometer (humidity gauge), this method will be quite sufficient. If your guitar is kept inside the case, I recommend either the "Damp–it®" or the "Planet Waves®" humidifier. Either of these humidifiers can be found in most music stores for between $12 and $16. It is still important to use a hygrometer to measure the humidity wherever your guitar is stored.

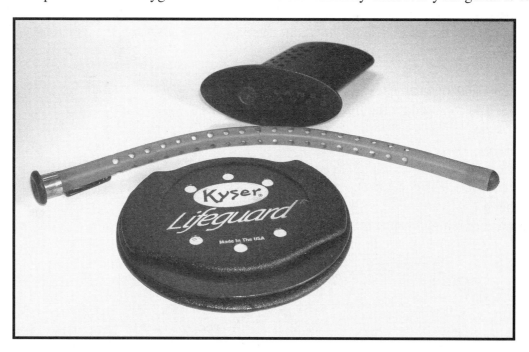

FIGURE 2.20 Here are a few of the different types of guitar humidifiers available on the market. (Photo by John LeVan)

Summary

To prolong the life of your guitar, here is what you need to remember:
1.   Hygiene (wash up before you play, wipe down the strings when finished playing)
2.   Clean and condition your guitar (0000 steel wool, lemon oil and guitar polish)
3.   Restring (strings should last about 20 - 30 playing hours if you keep them clean)
4.   Humidity and temperature (keep you guitar in a consistent environment)

This guide will help prevent premature wear and tear on your guitar and hopefully reduce costly visits to the repair shop.

Adjusting the Neck

This is the first step in a *setup*. A setup is a series of adjustments made to a guitar in order to maximize its playability. Adjusting the neck is a critical part of the entire process because, if it is done incorrectly, you will have to repeat the following steps in the setup procedure. Chapters 3 – 7 present the outline and process for doing a setup. If guitar doesn't have a trussrod, then you may skip this chapter

List of Components

The neck has several important components including:

1. Headstock (can be a multitude of shapes and sizes)
2. Tuning Keys (various colors and styles)
3. Trussrod Cover (not found on all guitars)
4. Trussrod Nut (this can be found at either end of the neck on different guitars)
5. String Nut (can be bone, metal, ivory, wood or plastic)
6. Fretboard (made of ebony, rosewood, maple, Micarta® or graphite)
7. Frets (nickel, silver and zinc alloy)
8. Trussrod (single-action, double-action or K-bar)
9. Trussrod Anchor (this can be found at either end of the neck in different guitars)
10. Neck Slab (maple, rosewood, graphite or mahogany)
11. Heel (where the neck attaches to the body)
12. String Trees (found on most but not all guitars) See figure 3.1

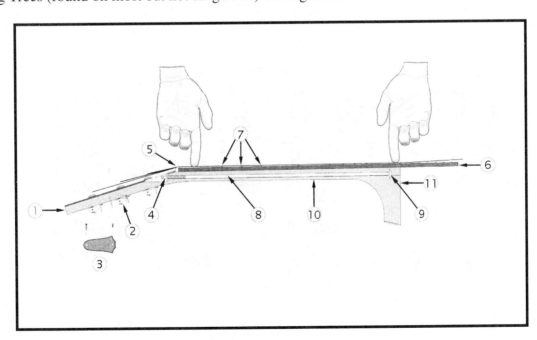

FIGURE 3.1 Here are the components of a guitar neck as listed above. (Illustration provided by the Taylor Guitar® Company)

An important aspect of guitar repair is the way in which you record measurements. The measurements you record will help you see the corrections you make as you work on your instrument. Throughout this book we will be recording many different measurements in order to compare the guitar before and after it has been setup. Here are a few foolproof techniques for sighting and adjusting the neck.

To measure the amount of relief (bow) in a neck:

1.   Tune the guitar to whatever pitch or tuning the player uses.
2.   Place a capo across the strings, directly over the first fret.
3.   Hold the guitar in playing position.
4.   Hold the low E string down at the (highest) last fret.
5.   Use your precision scale (ruler) or Action Gauge to measure the distance from the top of the frets to the bottom of the low E string at the middle of the neck
6.   Record the greatest distance between the frets and string

The first step in setting up any guitar is adjusting the neck. This step is critical because if the neck has too much forebow (inward or concave bow) and you adjust the action at the nut, you will need to replace the nut after you properly readjust the neck. The same is probable if you adjust the action at the bridge (on an acoustic guitar) before adjusting the neck. Unnecessary part replacement should be avoided. **The goal is to be accurate, efficient and effective.** Repeating steps will just waste time and energy. Before sighting the neck, make sure that the guitar is tuned to "concert pitch" (A-440) or whatever tuning the player uses. Next, sight the neck to check for either a backbow (convex) or a forebow (concave).

Three basic methods of sighting a neck:
1.   Visually looking down the neck from the headstock.
2.   Holding down the low E string at the 1st and 22nd fret.
3.   Setting a straightedge on top of the fingerboard.

Method No. 1 is great if you just want to "eyeball" the neck. However, it isn't very accurate for taking measurements. This technique will help you make a quick judgment as to whether the neck is fore-bowed or back-bowed.

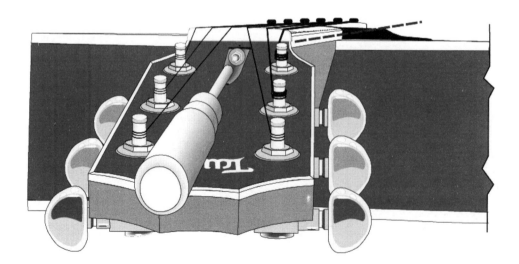

FIGURE 3.2 Holding the neck at the headstock, look down the fretboard to determine if the neck is fore-bowed or back-bowed. (Illustration provided by the Taylor Guitar® Company)

Method No. 2 is the easiest way to record an accurate measurement as long as the low E string is in good condition. *If it is bent or dented, your measurement will be inaccurate.* By placing a capo at the first fret and holding the low E string down at the last fret, or 14th on a acoustc, you can determine just how much forebow a neck has. If the neck is back-bowed, then you will not be able to record any measurements using this method.

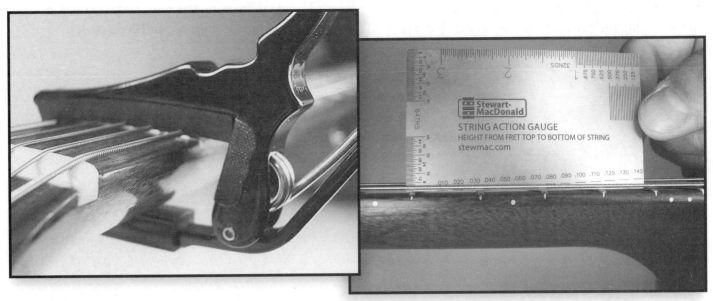

FIGURE 3.3A,B Note that the capo must be on top of the first fret, not in front of or behind it. 3.3B Hold the low E string down at the last fret and measure the greatest distance between the top of the fret to the bottom of the low E string. (Photos by John LeVan)

Method No. 3 is also a good technique to use when measuring the amount of relief in a neck. Even if the neck is *back-bowed* you can still measure the amount of backbow by holding the straightedge on top of the frets and measuring the distance between the bottom of the straightedge and the *top of the first (or last) fret*. The greater distance should be recorded. If the neck has a *forebow*, then hold the straightedge on top of the frets and measure the distance from the bottom of the straightedge to the *top of the frets in the middle of the neck.*

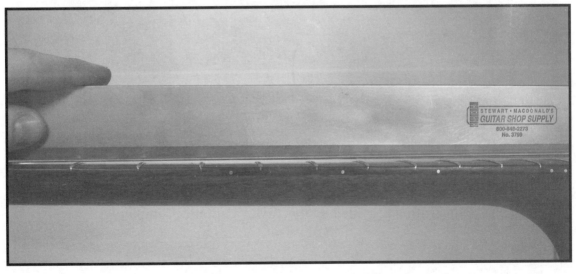

FIGURE 3.4 Method No. 3 is the same concept as method No. 2, however you are substituting the straightedge for low E string. When using method No. 3, be sure to place the straightedge between the D and G strings on top of the frets. As always, record the greatest distance between the top of the frets and the bottom of the straightedge. (Photo by John LeVan)

The Trussrod lies inside the neck. To adjust the neck, tighten or loosen the trussrod. By tightening the trussrod you force the neck to straighten or even backbow. When you loosen the trussrod, it releases the pressure and forebows or becomes concave. Turning the trussrod clockwise will tighten it and turning it counterclockwise will loosen it. If the neck is back-bowed, then loosen the rod; if the neck is fore-bowed, then tighten the rod. **When working on a vintage or old guitar you should always loosen the strings before tightening the trussrod.** If you don't, you risk stripping the rod and that's an expensive repair! **When in doubt, consult with a qualified luthier.**

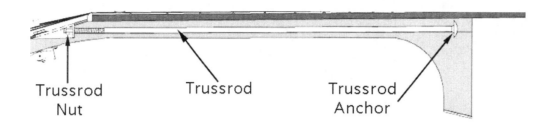

FIGURE 3.5 Here is a diagram of a trussrod, trussrod nut, and anchor. (Illustration provided by the Taylor Guitar® Company)

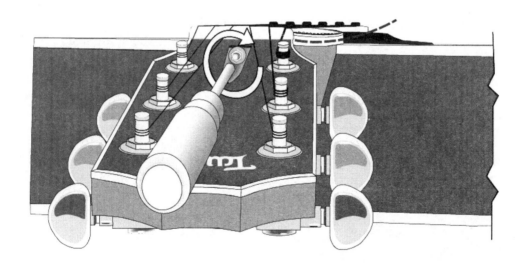

FIGURE 3.6 Here is a neck with too much forebow or too much relief. The trussrod needs to be tightened by turning it clockwise. (Illustration provided by the Taylor Guitar® Company)

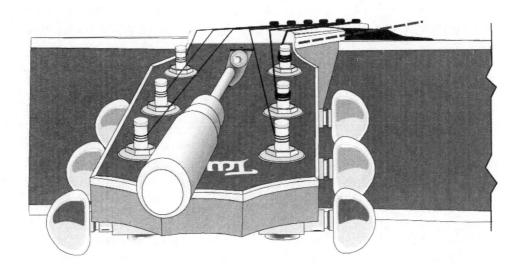

**FIGURE 3.7 Here is a correctly adjusted neck.
(Illustration provided by the Taylor Guitar® Company)**

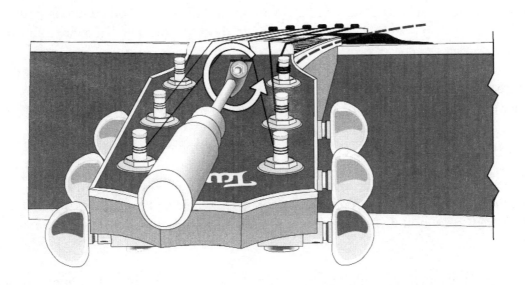

FIGURE 3.8 Here is a neck that is convex or back-bowed. The trussrod needs to be loosened by turning it counterclockwise. (Illustration provided by the Taylor Guitar® Company)

Most trussrods require a hex key, screwdriver or a nut driver (socket wrench). See illustrations above. There should be a slight amount of forebow in the neck, (approximately .010" to .020") depending on the instrument and condition of the neck. If the player wants fast and low action, .010" of relief is plenty. If the player uses a capo or is heavy handed, then .020" or more is recommended.

The trussrods in bass and electric guitars work the same way. Keep in mind that many bass guitars may need more relief (or bow) in the neck. Bass guitars have larger strings and are generally played more aggressively than other types of guitars.

This book will discuss the player/setup relationship in depth. *After all, the object of the exercise is to adjust the guitar to the player*. Knowing the style and technique of the player is critical to properly adjusting the guitar. Everyone has his or her own style and technique, that's why it's important to match the setup to the player.

There are two types of trussrods - adjustable and non-adjustable. Non-adjustable trussrods are also called K-bars or steel-reinforced rods. Adjustable trussrods come in two varieties - single and double-action.

Single-action trussrods force the neck in only one direction. As you tighten a single-action trussrod, it forces it to straighten or backbow the neck. When you loosen the rod it releases the pressure. Single action trussrods are used in most guitars. A common dilemma occurs when you have a neck that is back-bowed even after you have completely loosened the trussrod. To correct this problem you either have to replace the trussrod, or plane and refret the neck. Both repairs are expensive and require an experienced luthier.

Double-action trussrods force the neck in both directions. If the trussrod is loose and the neck is still back-bowed, then you keep turning it until it forces the neck in the other direction. Double-action trussrods are more stable and are usually found in finer guitars and basses.

Troubleshooting
As I mentioned earlier, trussrod repairs are difficult and expensive. In many cases it is more cost effective to buy a new neck than it is to repair a broken trussrod. There are several things that can go wrong with a trussrod. They can freeze or rust, break, strip or even cause the neck and fretboard to separate. Here are a few tips to identify a damaged trussrod:

- It spins freely when tightening
- It will not turn in either direction
- Rattles inside the neck when you play
- Has been run over by a car!

Occasionally, the only damage is that the trussrod nut has been stripped. If this is the case, then simply replace it and you're back in business. A new trussrod nut costs about $2. Whatever the case may be, if you are unsure, ask a professional. There is no substitute for experience, and nothing builds confidence like the experiences you will gain with time.

If the trussrod will not tighten, back off the trussrod nut and check to see if either the nut or rod is stripped. If the nut is stripped, replace it. If the rod is stripped, take the instrument to a qualified luthier.

Single Action Trussrod

Double Action Trussrod

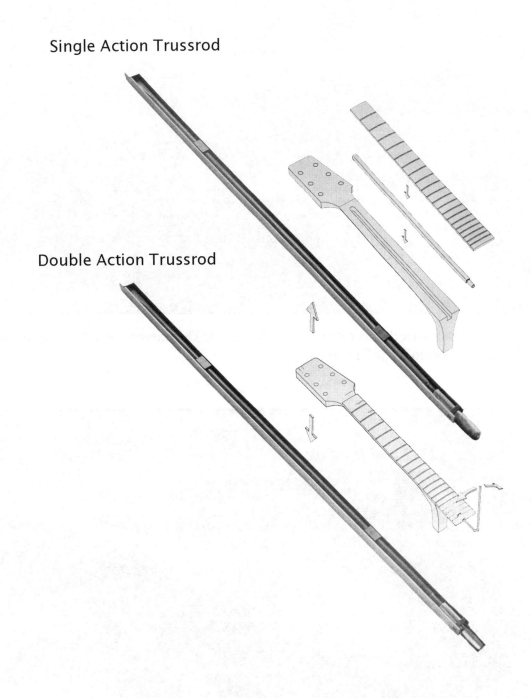

FIGURE 3.9 Single-action trussrods are common in most modern guitars. This type of trussrod forces the neck in only one direction. (Illustration by John LeVan)

FIGURE 3.10 Double-action trussrods can force the neck in two directions, thus making it easier to do set-ups and fretwork. (Illustration by John LeVan)

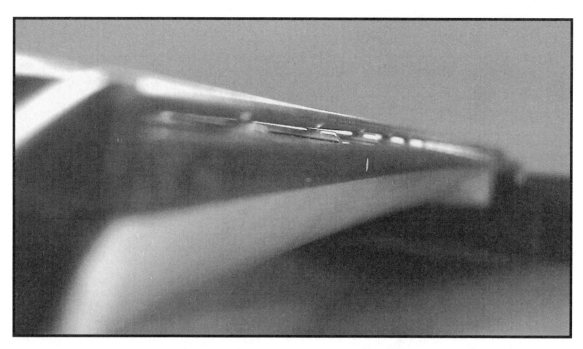

FIGURE 3.11 Here is a bass neck that is convex or back-bowed. The trussrod needs to be loosened by turning it counter clockwise. (Photo by John LeVan)

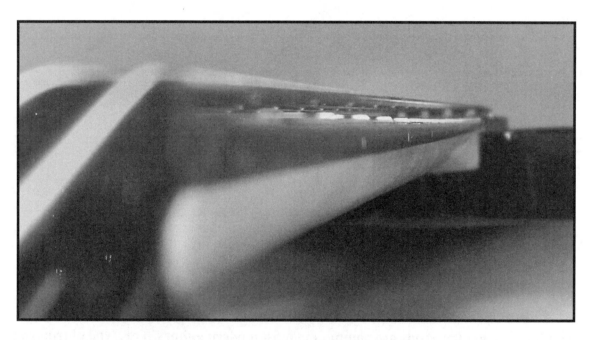

FIGURE 3.12 Here is a bass neck that has been properly adjusted. (Photo by John LeVan)

Adjusting the Action at the Bridge

Adjusting the action at the bridge is step two in the setup process. We adjust the string height at the bridge in order to make it easier to play the higher notes on the fretboard of the guitar. So far, we have done step one (adjusted the neck), and now we'll learn to do step two (adjust the height of the bridge).

Types of Bridges

* Acoustic Bridges
* Tunematic®
* Temolo Systems
* Hardtail Bridge
* Basses
* Dobro® and Resonator Guitars

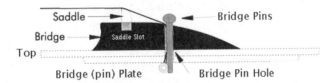

FIGURE 4.1 Acoustic guitar bridges come in many sizes and shapes, but generally contain the same components: Bridge saddle, saddle slot, bridge pins, pin holes (for the strings) and the bridge base. (Illustration provided by the Taylor Guitar® Company)

FIGURE 4.2 Tunematic® bridges are found on some electric guitars. They consist of a bridge base, bridge saddles, intonation adjustment screws, retention spring or wire, threaded inserts for the thumbwheels, and thumbwheels for height adjustment. (Photo by John LeVan)

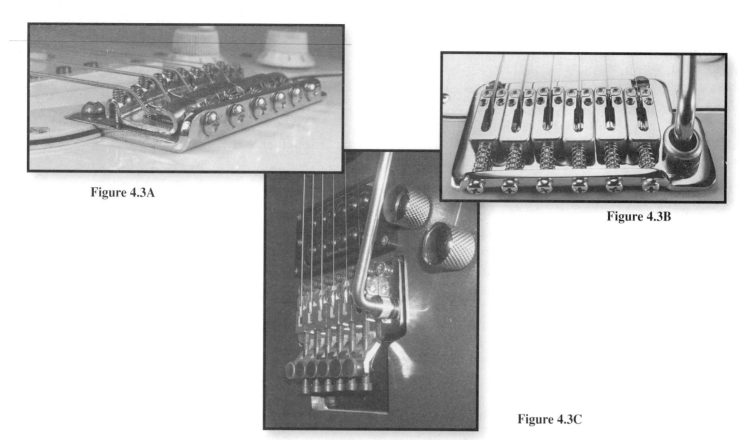

Figure 4.3A

Figure 4.3B

Figure 4.3C

FIGURE 4.3A There are several types of tremolo systems on the market. The most common are fulcrum style, single and double-locking, and Bigsby® style. (Photo by John LeVan) 4.3B They are composed of a base, tremolo arm (whammy bar), bridge saddles, saddle height adjustment screws, intonation adjustment screws, saddle locking screws, fine tuners, spring plate, inertia block, and tremolo arm spring. (Photo provided by L.R. Baggs®) 4.3C Notice that not all of these systems contain the same components. (Photo by John LeVan)

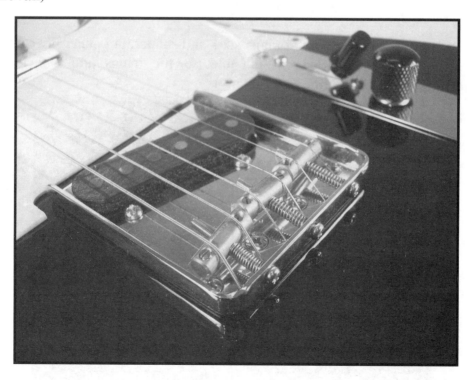

FIGURE 4.4 Hardtail bridges are common on Tele®-style electric guitars. Occasionally they are also found on Strat® style guitars as well. "Hardtail" refers to the fact that they are attached flush to the body and aren't a tremolo device. These bridges consist of bridge saddles, saddle height adjustment screws, intonation screws and springs, bridge plate and string ferrells. (Photo by John LeVan)

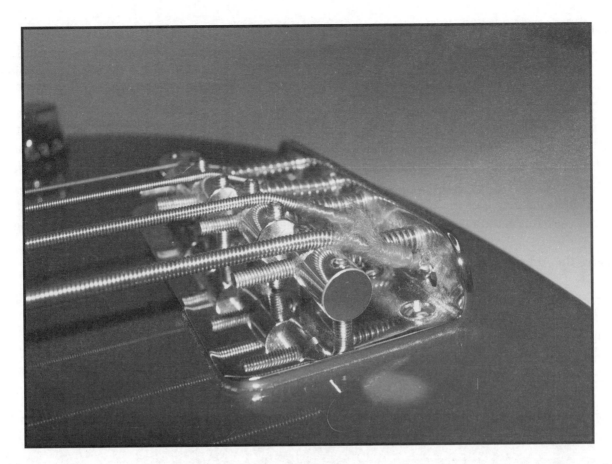

FIGURE 4.5 Bass guitars generally have a fixed bridge that attaches flush to the body (like a hardtail bridge). The components are the same with the exception of the number of saddles and the size of the components. (Photo by John LeVan)

FIGURE 4.6 Dobro® and Resonator guitars have a cone, biscuit, bridge saddle and a cover plate. Notice that the bridge saddle isn't radiused - instead it is flat or level on top.
(Photo by John LeVan)

The player's style is the deciding factor on the absolute height to follow. The strings should consistently graduate at least 1/64" from high E to low E. This will compensate for the difference in thickness in the strings. If every string were set at the same height, either the treble strings would be too high or the bass strings would tend to rattle.

The action at the bridge can be adjusted in several ways depending on the instrument. An electric guitar can be corrected by adjusting a thumbwheel or an Allen screw. An acoustic guitar is generally adjusted by sanding the bottom of the bridge saddle. One of the most important elements of a good setup is adjusting the guitar for the player's particular style. If the player is heavy-handed, the action (or distance of the strings to the frets) needs to be higher; if light-handed, then the action can be lower. If the action is too high, then the guitar can be difficult to play and can cause intonation problems. If too low, it can cause string rattle and dead spots on the string.

To Measure the Action at the Bridge

1. I recommend a well-machined scale (ruler) or Action Gauge® with good contrast that will measure to 1/64".
2. Place a capo over the strings on top of the first fret.
3. Measure the distance from the top of the 12th fret to the bottom of each string.
4. Record your measurement.

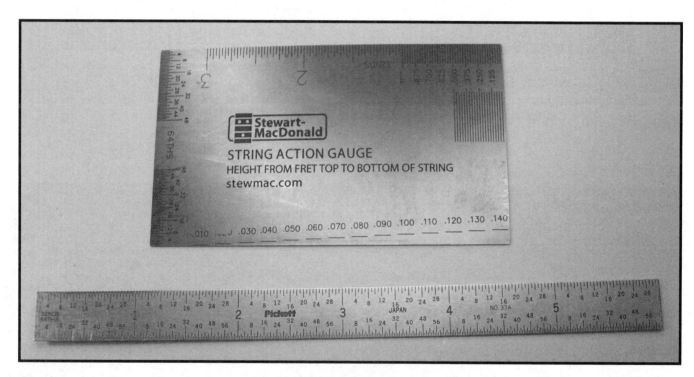

FIGURE 4.7 A good scale (ruler) to use is one that is 1/4" up to 6", with sharp contrast which makes it easy to read. The Stewart-MacDonald® Action Gauge® is an excellent tool. (Photo by John LeVan)

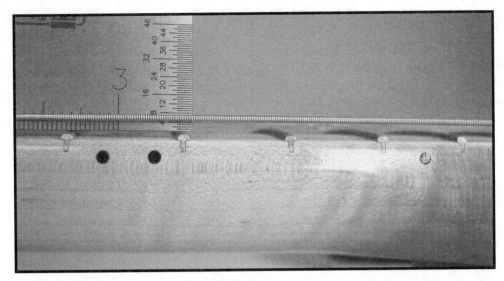

FIGURE 4.8 When measuring the action at the 12th fret, make sure your scale is level when you place it on top of the fret. It is also helpful to have a lot of light on the subject so that you can clearly see the measurements. (Photo by John LeVan)

Start with the high E and work your way to the low E. After you record the measurements for each string adjust the action of each string to the desired height. Keep in mind that you'll need to set the low E string approximately 1/64" higher than the high E string. All the other strings will graduate somewhere in between. The B string will be slightly higher than the high E, the G string will slightly higher than the B string, etc.

FIGURE 4.9 A gradual increase in the height of each string is the goal. If you raise the action too much, the guitar will be difficult to play, too little, and it will rattle and buzz. (Photo by John LeVan)

When adjusting the action of an acoustic guitar, remove the saddle from the bridge. Be sure to mark the bottom of the saddle, on both sides, with a mechanical pencil to show the amount of saddle you intend to remove. It is imperative to sand the saddle flush and square on the bottom to ensure a solid fit. This will also prevent any balancing problems if there is an under-saddle pickup. The best way I have found to do this is to use a flat surface (like a marble slab or counter top) and self-adhesive sandpaper (220 grit). Sand the saddle away from yourself in one direction. With the saddle in an upright position, push it across the sandpaper. Always sand the saddle in one direction - away from yourself. The object of the exercise is to keep consistent pressure on the saddle so that it ends up perfectly flat and square on the bottom. If you fail to keep the saddle perpendicular to the sandpaper, the saddle will be uneven and result in tone loss and uneven string balance. Check the saddle periodically to ensure that you don't remove too much at a time. Like the other types of guitars, you should leave a height difference of about 1/64" from low E to high E. Keep in mind that if the saddle is not compensated (intonated), then you may need to leave it about 1/64" tall so it doesn't end up too low after you set the intonation. A reasonable height for an acoustic is 4/64" on the treble and 5/64" on the bass side when measuring at the 12th fret (with a capo on the first fret). It is also important that the radius of the top of the saddle match the radius of the fretboard, this will give the action a consistent and gradual increase from the high E string to the low E string.

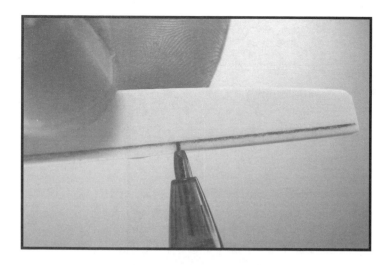

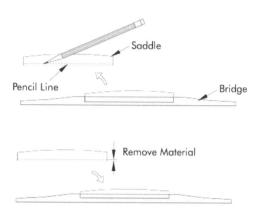

FIGURE 4.10 Carefully mark the bottom of the saddle. A mechanical pencil works great. I recommend marking both sides of the saddle so you can see if you are sanding it flat or if you are tilting to one side or the other. (Photo by John LeVan)

FIGURE 4.11 Sand the bridge saddle square and flat on the bottom. If you tilt it while sanding, the saddle won't be flush to the saddle slot. This can a problem if the guitar has an under-saddle pickup. (Illustration provided by the Taylor Guitar® Company)

From time to time, you will encounter a guitar with a Tunematic® bridge (Les Paul® or SG® type) that has inconsistent string height and incorrect string spacing. In this case, it is recommended that you either re-cut the saddles (using nut files) or replace the bridge altogether. If the bridge looks as though it is sinking in the middle, it needs to be replaced.

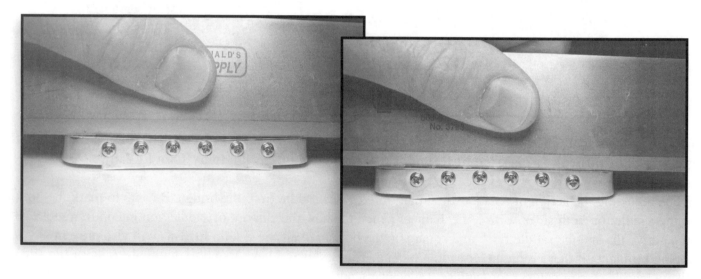

FIGURE 4.12A,B Note the difference between a sinking bridge on the left and a good bridge on the right. This is a common problem with this style of bridge. In addition, the spacing on the sinking bridge is inconsistent while the good bridge has accurate string spacing. Accurate spacing will make the guitar easier to play. (Photos by John LeVan)

To adjust a Strat®, Tele®-style or bass bridge, use a hex key set. The sizes can differ for each guitar from .05" to 1.5mm, but the basics remain the same. Remember that it is important to make sure that the saddle is level after you adjust it. Like all skills, practice makes perfect. To raise the saddle, turn the hex screw clockwise. To lower the saddle, turn the hex screw counterclockwise. A reasonable action for an electric guitar is 2/64" on the treble side and 3/64" on the bass side (measuring at the 12th fret with a capo on the first fret). For an aggressive player raise the action 1/64" to compensate for the players playing style.

FIGURE 4.13 These types of saddles are adjusted by two hex screws. It is important to keep them level with the bridge plate. It may play ok, but if they aren't level your setup will not look very professional. (Photo by Skip Anderson)

To adjust a tremolo-style bridge, you may need hex keys and a Phillips or flathead screwdriver. Make sure to know whether to adjust the tremolo flush to the body of the guitar or with a certain amount of "draw." "Draw" refers to the increments of notes you can pull sharp using the tremolo bar. Some players prefer a flush mount bridge for doing double-stop bends, etc. Some prefer a half–to- whole-note draw to accent a solo or chord. Adjusting the tremolo springs in the back of the guitar does this. The tremolo springs are adjusted by (tightening and loosening) the screws on the claw. With each adjustment, tune the guitar to pitch and retest the amount of draw. To adjust the tremolo flush to the body, tighten the screws on the claw. To float the tremolo, loosen the screws on the claw. It may take several attempts to get it right. IT IS VERY IMPORTANT TO RETUNE THE GUITAR TO THE CORRECT PITCH EACH TIME YOU MAKE AN ADJUSTMENT. Otherwise, you will end up with the tremolo positioned forward (not level) rendering the guitar unplayable.

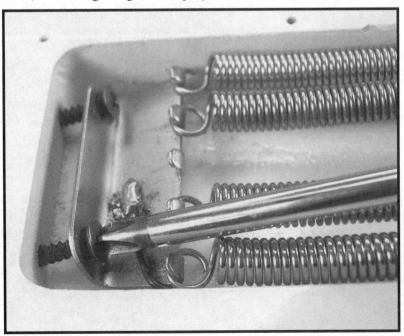

FIGURE 4.14 Regardless of what tool you need to adjust this type of bridge, it's important that you set it up to accommodate the player's style. Whether the player wants to draw the bridge back, or will never use the whammy bar, make sure that the spring claw is adjusted for that style of play. (Photo by John LeVan)

Classical guitars have nylon strings and are played very dynamically. As a result, the action needs to be higher than the average acoustic. These guitars are usually fingerpicked using fingernails instead of guitar picks. As with any acoustic or electric, make sure that the top of the saddle matches the radius of the fretboard. A reasonable action for a classical is 6/64" on the treble side and 7/64" on the bass side measuring at the 12th fret with a capo on the first fret.

FIGURE 4.15A,B Adjust the saddle the same way as an acoustic, but keep the action higher to accommodate the player's style of play. (Photos by John LeVan)

Dobro® and resonator guitars require high action because they are played with either a slide or bar. As a result, the tops of the strings need to be at the same height or action. To adjust the action correctly, you need to measure it differently than the other types of guitars. For a Dobro® or resonator, measure from the top of the 12th fret to the top of each string. All the strings should be set at the same height. 7/64" to 9/64" at the 12th fret is reasonable for a Dobro® or resonator.

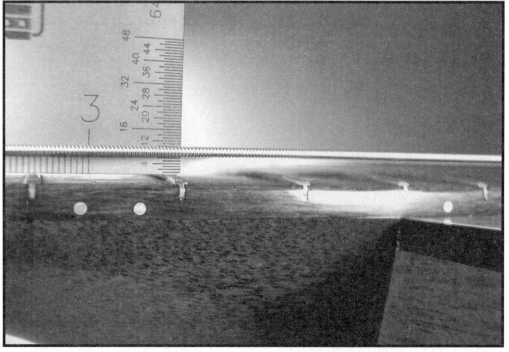

FIGURE 4.16 The tops of the strings should be level with each other. Otherwise, not all of the strings will be heard when you use a slide or bar to play it. (Photo by John LeVan)

Neck angle issues can really complicate matters and this applies to all guitars. In this example, we are using a guitar with a tremolo system. Below are a few examples of the common symptoms of an incorrect neck angle:

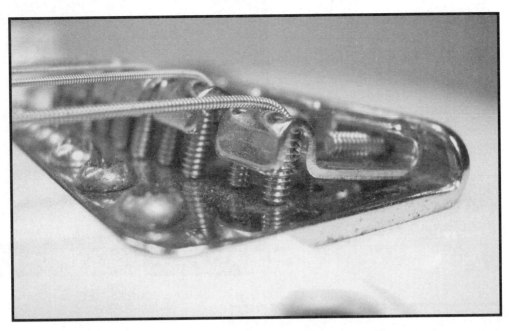

FIGURE 4.17 Tremolo is flush to body, bridge saddles are adjusted as high as possible, but action is still too low. This is an example of a guitar with a high or overset neck angle. (Photo by John LeVan)

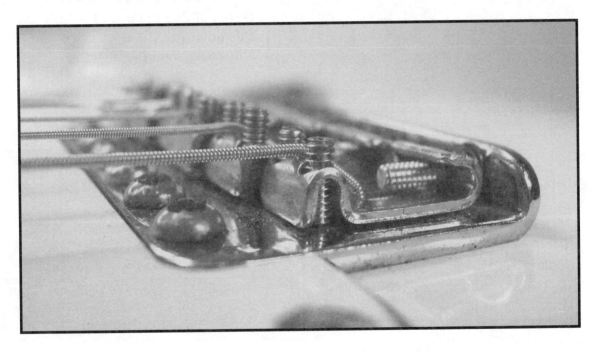

FIGURE 4.18 Tremolo is flush to body, bridge saddles are adjusted as low as possible, but action is too high. Here is a guitar with a low or underset neck angle. (Photo by John LeVan)

To correct this problem on an electric guitar is fairly simple. Place an angled shim under the neck to tilt it to the correct angle. It is critically important to use a shim that is the same size as the neck pocket. Just throwing a pick under the neck is not a good idea because it can cause the neck to warp where it bolts onto the body. As for an acoustic guitar, unless it has a bolt-on neck, changing the neck angle is time consuming and expensive. Only a qualified, factory-authorized luthier should attempt this adjustment.

FIGURE 4.19 If the shim doesn't fully cover the pocket, it can result in tone loss and a warped neck. (Photo by John LeVan)

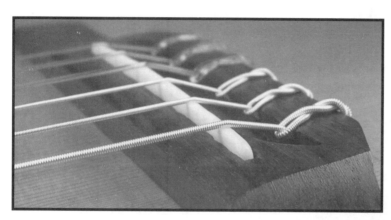

FIGURE 4.20 For a classical guitar a gradual increase in the height of each string is the goal. If you raise the action too much, the guitar will be too difficult to play. Too little and it will rattle and buzz.
(Photo by John LeVan)

FIGURE 4.21 When adjusting a classical, keep the action high enough to accomodate the player's style of play.
(Photo by John LeVan)

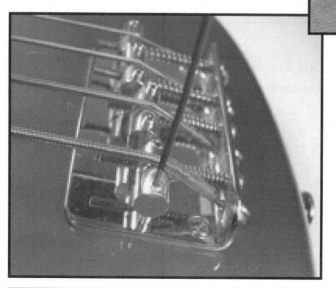

FIGURE 4.22 These types of saddles are adjusted by two hex screws. It is important to keep them level with the bridge plate. It may play ok, but if they aren't level your setup will not look very professional. (Photo by John LeVan)

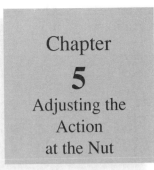

Adjusting the Action at the Nut

Adjusting the action at the nut is step three of a setup. This is a very important part of a setup because if the action is too high at the nut, the guitar will be difficult to play and will not play in tune. High action at the nut is usually needed only when the player is using a slide.

So far we have done step one (adjusting the neck) and step two (adjusting the action at the bridge); now we will do step three (adjusting the action at the nut).

Diagram of Components

String Nut
- String Slots
- String Angles
- Slot Width
- String Spacing

FIGURE 5.1 Here is an illustration of the string nut. (Photo by John LeVan)

Tools Needed:
- Nut Files
- Scale (Miniature Metal Ruler)
- Action Gauge® by Stewart-MacDonald®

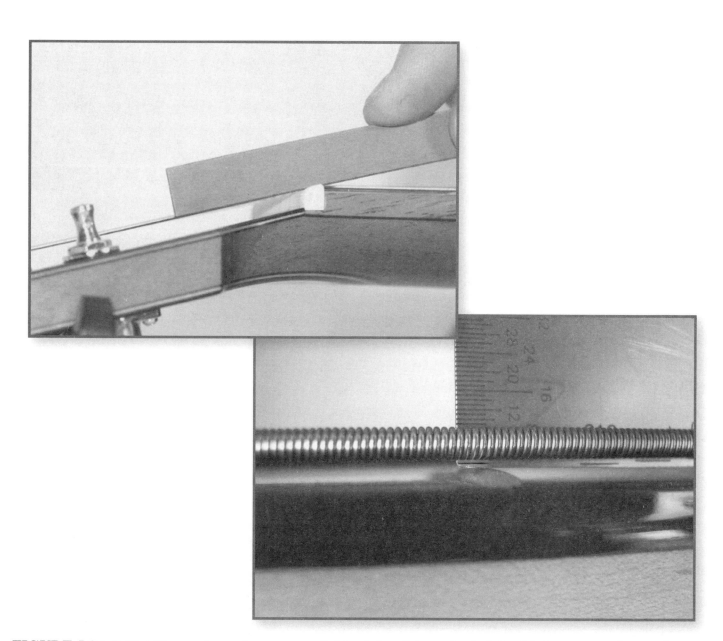

FIGURE 5.2A,B Nut files and a scale are essential to doing this project right. Make sure to choose the correct nut files for the guitar you are working on, and in particular, for the gauge of strings being used on it. The Stewart-Macdonald® Action Gauge® is a perfect tool to measure the action at the nut. Be sure to measure from the top of the first fret to the bottom of the string. (Photo 5.2B by John Levan) (Photo 5.2A by Skip Anderson)

A proven way to adjust the string height at the nut is to use a set of nut files. I recommend at least 10 different sizes:

- .010
- .012
- .016
- .022
- .026
- .032
- .036
- .040
- .046
- .052
- A set of round needle files for bass guitars

Angles, Width and Spacing

It is critically important to cut the nut slots at the correct angle, width and spacing. The *angle* of the slot should match the angle of the string from the front of the nut to the tuning key peg. If the slot angle is incorrect, then the string will either rattle or not intonate properly. If the string slot is not cut to the proper width, then it can cause tuning problems, string breakage and string rattle. The *width* of the slot is equally important. When the slot is too narrow the string will bind in the slot and can break as well as cause tuning problems. If the slot is cut too wide, the string will rattle and buzz when played in the open position. String *spacing* is the distance from one string to another. If there is a greater space between the B and G string than between the A and low E string, then the spacing is incorrect. This can make the guitar difficult to play. Measuring from the outside edges of the strings, all of the strings should be the same distance from each other.

FIGURE 5.3 Be sure to cut the string slot at the same angle as the string from the face of the nut to the end of the tuning key peg. (Photo by John LeVan)

Never cut the slot more that 2/1000" over the width of the string. Equally as important is to avoid cutting the slot too narrow.

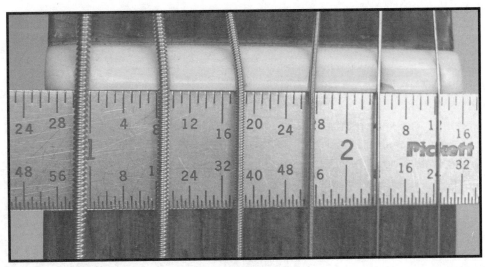

FIGURE 5.4 String spacing is also important. If the spacing is off, it can cause the E strings to slip off of the neck when you play. (Photo by John LeVan)

Proper Adjustments

All proper adjustments begin with accurate measurements.

To measure the action at the nut, tune the guitar to pitch, and place your rule or Stewart-MacDonald® Action Gauge® on top of the first fret at the high E string. Record the distance from the top of the fret to the bottom of the string. Generally you need about 1/64" or 15/1000" distance from the top of the fret to the bottom of the string for the high E string. For the low E string double the distance. *Keep in mind that the actual height will ultimately be determined by the player's style. If the player is heavy-handed, you need to add about .010" of height.* **The low E should be slightly higher than the high E by at least 1/64"**. The rest of the strings should be an ascending balance between the two E strings. In other words, the B string will be slightly higher than the high E string, the G will be slightly higher than the B string, etc,. **It may take a while to train your eye to see such small detail, but like all skills, practice makes perfect. This is the same formula used in Chapter 4 on adjusting the action at the bridge.**

For a classical guitar you will need to double the string height, in other words the high E will be 2/64" or 30/1000" from the top of the fret to the bottom of the string. The low E will need to be 3/64" or 45/1000" from the top of the fret to the bottom of the string. Because classical strings have less tension than steel strings, they tend to rattle and buzz more when played. It is also common for classical players to play more dynamically and aggressively than steel-string players.

Bass guitars tend to have higher action at the bridge than the other steel-stringed guitars mentioned in this chapter. Because they are tuned to a lower octave, the action should be higher than the other guitars, but the action at the nut is the same. I recommend adjusting the action at the nut as follows; the G string should be no less than 1/64" or 15/1000" from the top of the first fret to the bottom of the string. The E should be no less than 2/64" or 30/1000" from the top of the fret to the bottom of the string. Remember that these measurements are done on top of the first fret. Be aware of the playing style of the player. If they are heavy-handed, you'll need to add at least .010" to the height of the strings at the nut.

Dobro® and slide guitars require very high action. Because they are played with either a slide or a metal bar, the action should be adjusted differently than a guitar that is fingered when played. *The tops of all the strings should be the same height from the tops of the frets.* This is different from the other types of guitars because they are measured from the top of the fret to the bottom of the strings, but with a slide guitar you need the strings to be the same action on the top of the string not the bottom. The reason for this is because the slide or bar used to play the guitar is usually flat. So, in order to get clean contact, the strings must be the same height. To accomplish this task, you need to measure from the top of the fret to the top of the strings and adjust them to the same height. Keep in mind that the rules about the nut slot angles, width and distance still apply.

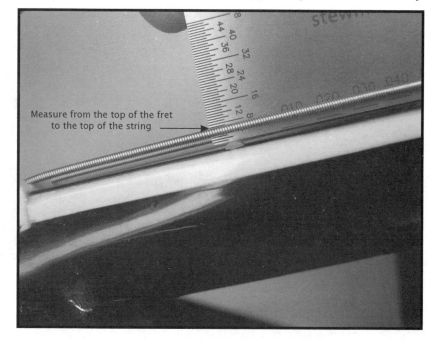

Measure from the top of the fret to the top of the string

FIGURE 5.5 Dobro® and slide guitars are the only styles of guitars that require that the action match from the top of the fret to the top of each string. (Photo by John LeVan)

Replacement and Repair

There are times when you just need a quick fix, and there are times when you need a permanent repair. A quick fix is acceptable when you're on the road or don't have the time and resources for a permanent repair. Filling the nut is a quick fix and a temporary repair. You should replace the nut as soon as possible if it's worn or cut too low. Below are some common problems and some quick fixes and permanent solutions.

When the string slot is cut too low. The strings will rattle on the open notes; this is often called the **SITAR EFFECT**. There are two ways to fix this problem.

> **1. Fill the string slot with a material that is the same as what the nut is made of**
> **2. Replace the nut**

If you don't have the resources to replace the nut, then the next best thing is to fill the slot and re-cut it. This is only a temporary fix until you can replace it.

TO REPAIR / FILL NUT SLOT

- Clean out the slot removing any dirt, graphite or glue
- Next, fill the slot with either bone or plastic dust [whatever material the nut is made of]
- Add a drop of Super Glue® to seal and bond the dust into the slot
- Spray Super Glue® Accelerator onto the slot (glue will dry immediately)
- Re-cut the slot to the correct depth

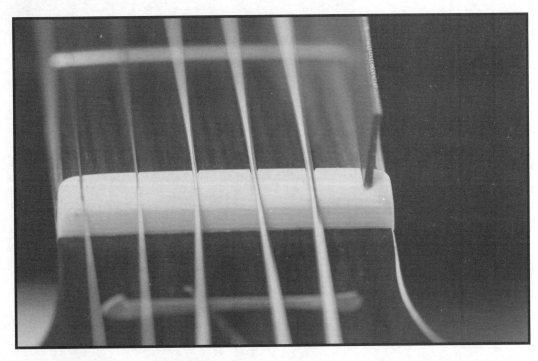

FIGURE 5.6 Clean out the slot using a nut file. You may want to use a file that is slightly larger than the slot for this. (Photo by Skip Anderson)

FIGURE 5.7A,B Loosely pack the slot with a like material to the nut. If the nut is bone, use bone. (Photos by Skip Anderson)

FIGURE 5.8 Apply one drop of thin Super Glue® to the slot. Always have a Q-Tip® in your hand when working with Super Glue®. Use the Q-Tip® to absorb any excess glue before it can drip onto the finish. (Photo by Skip Anderson)

Spray a little bit of Super Glue® Accelerator into the slot to speed up the drying process.

FIGURE 5.9 Re-cut the string slot to the correct width, depth and angle. (Photo by Skip Anderson)

To replace the nut, lightly tap the front of the nut with the tip of a flathead screwdriver to break it loose. If this doesn't work try a drop of solvent. Make sure you don't get any of the solvent on the finish of the neck, solvent can melt the finish of most guitars. Then clean out the nut slot with a miniature file to remove all the glue before you install the new nut. Be certain that the nut fits snug and flush. Using a drop of thin Super Glue® between the D and G string, secure it to the end of the fingerboard. Re-cut the string slots to the proper action as per the instructions at the beginning of this chapter. This procedure is discussed in detail in chapter 11.

Adjusting the Pickups

Adjusting the pickups is step four of a setup. If done properly, your pickups will sound full and balanced. If done incorrectly, your guitar will sound unbalanced and can develop string rattle and intonation problems. At this point you should have completed step one (adjusting the trussrod), step two (adjusting the bridge), and step three (adjusting the nut). Now we'll perform step four (adjusting the pickups).

List of Components:
- Pickups
- Strings
- Pickup Height Adjustment Screws

FIGURE 6.1A,B The screws on each side of the pickup are used to adjust its height in relationship to the strings. (Photos by John LeVan)

Proper Height and Effects

The purpose of adjusting the pickups is to ensure equal volume from each string. The adjustment can also minimize fret buzz and intonation problems. *This is done on magnetic pickups only*. Pickup adjustment is done by changing the height of the pickup, in relationship to the strings. If the pickup height is too high, it can cause string buzz and intonation problems due to the magnetic pull of the pickup on the strings. If the pickups are too low, it causes a weak signal and unbalanced string volume.

Proper adjustment is dependent upon the height of the pickup in relationship to the string. Generally, the bridge pickup can be closer to the string than the other pickups. This is because that location of the string is least likely to be pulled out of intonation by the magnets in the pickups. The strings are not as stable at the middle and neck positions.

Pickup height can vary from 3/32" to 6/32" from pickup to pickup. I generally set the pickup at 3/32" at the treble side and 4/32" at the bass side. I don't recommend setting the pickups any higher than this because it can cause the magnetic poles on the pickup to pull on the string. The most accurate way to measure the pickup height is to hold the string down at the last fret and measure the height of the strings at the pickups on the high and low E strings. From there, test the string balance by playing the guitar and listening to the volume of each string from pickup to pickup, adjusting the height of the pickups accordingly.

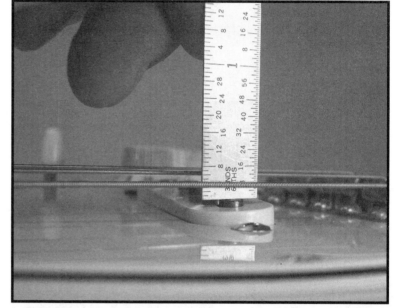

FIGURE 6.2 Measure from the top of the magnet to the bottom of the string (while you hold the strings down at the last fret).
(Photo by John LeVan)

FIGURE 6.3 Measure from the top of the magnet to the bottom of the string. For bass guitars, I recommend a height of 5/32" at the treble side and 6/32" at the bass side (while you hold the strings down at the last fret). You may need to lower the pickups a bit more if the player uses a slap style of playing, to prevent the strings from striking the pickups.
(Photo by John LeVan)

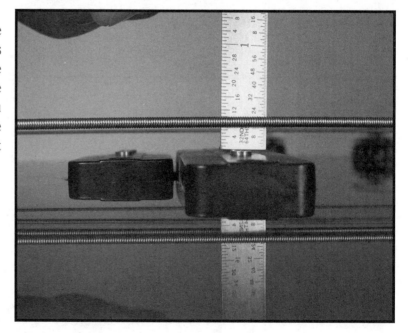

Setting the Intonation

S etting the intonation is step five of a setup. Without setting the intonation, the guitar will never play even close to in tune. So far we have completed step one (adjusting the neck), step two (adjusting the action at the bridge), step three (adjusting the action at the nut), and step four (adjusting the pickups). In step five we'll set the intonation.

Intonation means to sound in perfect unison. The purpose of intonating a guitar is to make it play in tune both with itself and with other properly intonated instruments. Understanding the fundamentals and variables of intonation is crucial to the performance of any guitar. Even the best guitars are useless if they don't play in tune. Learning to intonate and temper an instrument are skills that you will learn in this chapter. We will define, test and discuss variables and temperaments and how to balance them to the instrument as well as the player.

Tools Needed

There are many different types of guitar bridges. Therefore, you will need several types of tools including:

- Hex Keys
- Flathead Screwdrivers
- Phillips Screwdrivers
- Miniature Flat Files
- Guitar Tuner

FIGURE 7.1 Choose the right tool for the job. The hex keys and screwdrivers are generally used for electric guitars and basses. The miniature flat file is used to intonate an acoustic. (Photo by Skip Anderson)

As discussed in Chapter 4, most electric guitar bridges are adjusted with either a screwdriver or hex keys. The screw or hex bolt in the rear of the bridge allows you to adjust the bridge saddle back and forth. Changing the position of the bridge saddle will change the intonation of that string.

To adjust the intonation on an acoustic guitar, the bridge saddle must be carved into the proper position for each string with a miniature flat file. When intonating an acoustic bridge saddle be very careful to carve the angles at the correct pitch. If you carve a saddle too steep, it will result in string breakage, tone loss, volume loss and tuning problems. If you carve it too shallow, the string may rattle over the bridge saddle and the instrument will also lose tone and volume.

FIGURE 7.2 Be sure to carve the saddle to the correct angle with your mini flat file. Take special care not to slip and scratch the bridge or the top. A piece of cardboard or pickgaurd material is a wise choice to use as a shield or guard during this process. (Photo by John LeVan)

Testing
Before you set the intonation, be sure that the following four steps have been completed in order:

1. Adjust the neck
2. Adjust the action at the bridge
3. Adjust the action at the nut
4. Adjust the pickups (where applicable)

Once the guitar is in tune (using a guitar tuner) and the strings are settled and holding their tune, check the 12th fret harmonic against the fretted note at the 12th fret. Make sure that you read the *attack* of the note not the *drift* when using your tuner. The *attack* is the immediate reaction of the note; *drift* occurs as the note settles. The goal is to match the harmonic tone with the fretted note. THE HARMONIC IS ALWAYS TRUE, SO THAT IS YOUR <u>CONSTANT</u> OR CONTROL NOTE. THE FRETTED NOTE IS ALWAYS THE <u>VARIABLE</u>. It is very important to use an accurate tuner for adjusting the intonation. A Saunderson Accutuner® or a Strobe tuner is the best type of tuner on the market at present.

Sharp, Flat and Hopeless? Now that you have established whether the fretted note is either sharp (♯) or flat (♭), it's time to adjust the intonation for each saddle. If the fretted note is sharp (♯) then the saddle for that string needs to be moved away from the neck (back). If the fretted note is flat (♭) then the saddle needs to move towards the neck (forward). Sharp (♯) means the string is too short; flat (♭) means the string is too long.

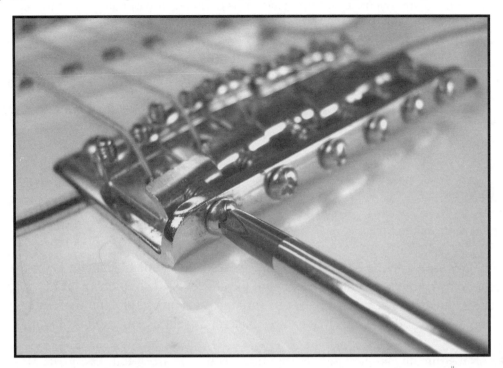

FIGURE 7.3 On an electric guitar, tighten the intonation screw if the note is sharp (♯). If the note is flat (♭), loosen the screw. (Photo by Skip Anderson)

When intonating an acoustic, the bridge saddle must be carved for each string as each string has its own angle. If the angle for each string is not carved correctly, it can result in tuning problems, string breakage, tone loss, volume loss and cracks in the bridge saddle. The string angle should follow the angle from the bridge pin to the end of the intonation point on the saddle (similar to the angle on the string nut).

FIGURE 7.4 Use a mini flat file to carve the intonation points to the correct location on the bridge saddle. (Photo by Skip Anderson)

Bridge saddles are made from many different materials such as, bone, ivory, Micarta®, Tusq and plastic. Each material has a specific sound and longevity. Bone and ivory tend to last the longest and sound the best.

Variables and tempering need to be identified and understood in order to control them. A critical variable to intonating is the string nut. If the front of the nut is worn or chipped, it can cause the intonation to be sharp (♯). Likewise, raising and lowering the height of the bridge saddle will effect the intonation. This is why intonating is the last step in a setup.

Other variables include:
- Worn Frets
- Inaccurate Fret Placement
- Inaccurate Nut Placement
- Inaccurate Bridge Saddle Placement
- Pick Size
- Velocity of Strum
- Fret Height
- How Hard You Press the Strings

One of the most widely used calculations to determine nut, fret and saddle placement is the *Rule of 18*. The Rule of 18 is rather complicated, however, if the placement of the above listed components is not correct, the guitar will never play in tune. Six out of seven of the above listed variables are correctable, fret placement is not cost effective to correct. However, there are adjustments that can be made to offset this common problem.

Believe it or not, no instrument can play perfectly in tune. Thus, the art of tempering was developed. *Tempering* is the balancing of tones to make an instrument sound more pleasing to the ear. In other words, each string on a guitar is intonated and tuned slightly off pitch in order to make most chords sound in tune. Pianos are commonly temper-tuned in order to play in tune with themselves. Likewise, a guitar can also be temper-tuned. This practice dates back to the time of Bach when he nearly lost his head because he subverted tradition by temper-tuning his piano. By adjusting the intonation screws on the bridge saddles (on most guitars), you can easily temper them to sound more pleasing.

On an acoustic guitar the B and low E strings tend to sound sharp (♯). I recommend intonating the low E at the 3rd fret. In other words, tune the string using the corresponding 12th fret harmonic (control note) and then play the note at the 3rd fret (variable note). If the note at the 3rd fret measures exactly G on your tuner, then you're finished with that string. If the note is sharp (♯), then file the saddle on the front or neck side to lengthen the string. If flat (♭), then the string is too long and the saddle needs to be filed on the backside. Next, intonate the rest of the strings at the 12th fret.

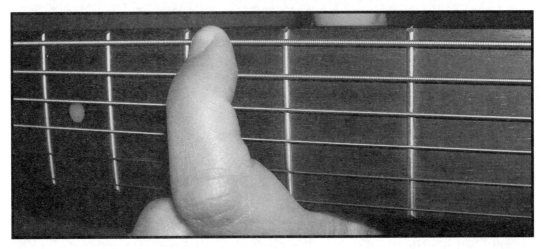

FIGURE 7.5 After tuning the guitar to the desired pitch, fret the low E string at the third fret and check to see if the note (G) is in tune. Then adjust the saddle as needed. The goal is for the note (G) to be in tune with the tuner. (Photo by John LeVan)

As far as electric guitars go, the G string is the biggest problem compounded by the high E string. Keep in mind we are talking about a guitar with a plain G string, not a wound G string. For a guitar with a plain G string, I *intonate all but the high E and G at the 12th fret*. Intonate the high E at the 3rd fret like the low E on an acoustic. Then I play the G string at the15th fret and compare it with the open D string. I then intonate or adjust the length of the G string by ear (sounds frightening huh?) until it sounds in tune with the open A and D strings. I don't use a guitar tuner for intonating the G string because, even though the tuner shows that the G is intonated, it won't sound in tune on several of the commonly played chords. *Make sure you retune after every adjustment*. I know it sounds complicated, but this is the best system I have found without making permanent modifications like relocating the string nut or the bridge.

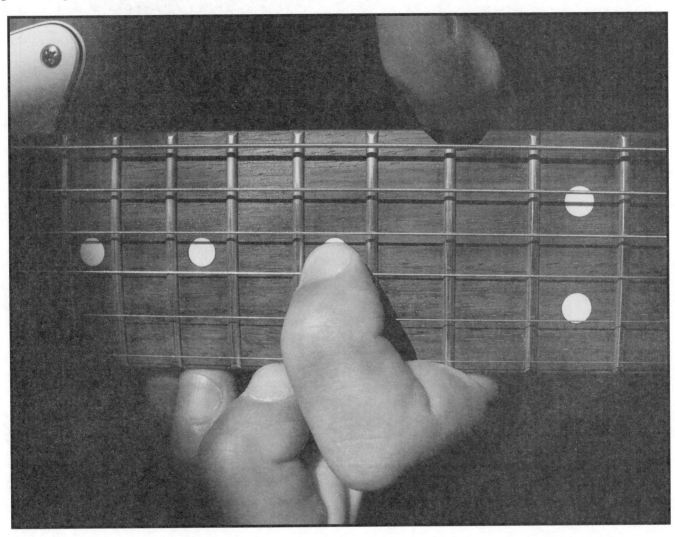

FIGURE 7.6 After tuning the guitar to the desired pitch, fret the G string at the 15th fret and check to see if the note is in tune with the open A and D strings. Then adjust the saddle as needed.
(Photo by John LeVan)

FIGURE 7.7 On a bass guitar, tighten the intonation screw if the note is sharp (♯). If the note is flat (♭) loosen the screw. (Photo by John LeVan)

Classical and bass guitars are generally intonated using the traditional method of matching the 12th fret harmonic with the fretted note at the 12th fret. This completes the setup process. At this point we have completed all five steps: 1.adjusting the neck, 2. adjusting the action at the bridge, 3. adjusting the action at the nut, 4. adjusting the pickups and finally, step five - setting the intonation. Your guitar should now play better than ever, and who knows? Maybe someday you'll be a rock star!

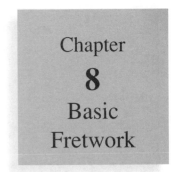

Basic Fretwork

Fretwork is an art that requires skill, patience and good tools. It takes many years of practice and study to become proficient at fretwork. The most important skills to develop are accurate hand/eye coordination, consistent and repetitious motor skills and the ability to clearly see light as it reflects off of a fret.

List of Components
- Leveling Bar
- Frets and Fretwire
- Buckshot
- Trough (Optional)
- Straightedges
- Recrowning Files
- Sandpaper
- Super Glue®
- Q-Tips®
- Fretting Hammer
- Flush-Cut Dykes (Large)
- Flush-Cut Dykes (Small)
- Fret Tang Nippers
- X-Acto® Knife
- Soldering Iron
- Drill Press Vise
- Bench Cover
- Brass Wire Brush
- Good Lighting

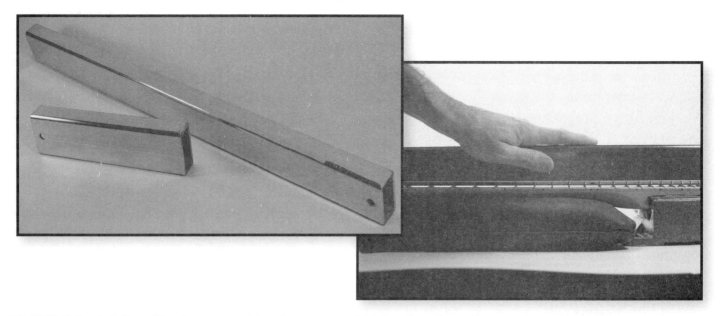

FIGURE 8.1A,B Leveling bar is used for (you guessed it) leveling frets. It must be perfectly flat on two sides and be at least 1" wide. (Photos by Skip Anderson)

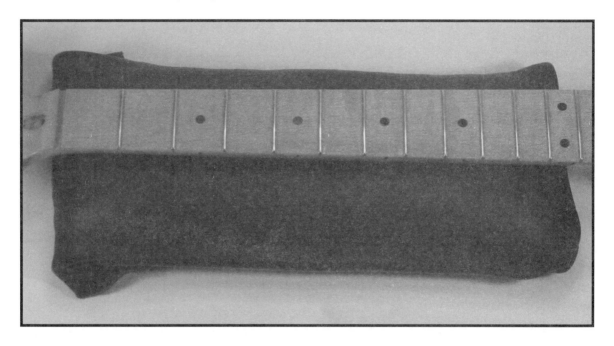

FIGURE 8.2 Buckshot should be in an airtight, sealed, bag. Buckshot is usually made from lead, so it's important to keep it contained. I use a 25-pound bag of No. 6 shot contained in a sealed leather bag. This is used to support the neck to keep it from shifting or flexing. (Photo by Skip Anderson)

I learned the value of buckshot when I studied at the Taylor® Guitar factory in El Cajon, CA. They used a 25-pound bag to rest the neck of a guitar on when leveling the frets. This kept the neck from flexing during leveling and the fretting hammer from bouncing back when installing the frets. I found that sealing the bag of shot in leather prevents contact with the potentially dangerous lead dust.

Troughs can be made from wood and should be open at both ends. The sealed bag of buckshot is placed into the trough when doing fretwork on an acoustic guitar.

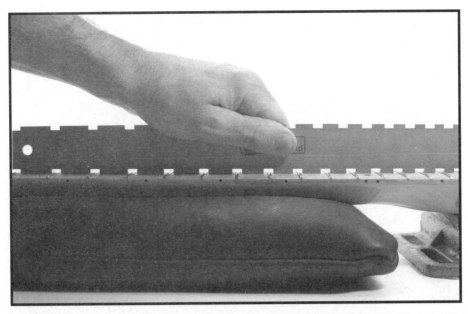

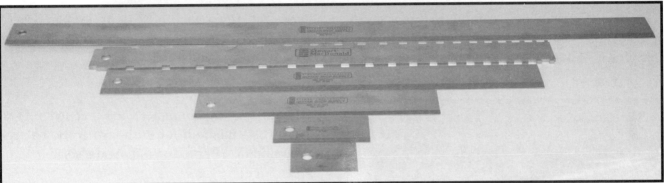

FIGURE 8.3A,B Straightedges are critical to doing good fretwork. I recommend two kinds of straight-edges, notched and unnotched. Notched straightedges are designed to reveal how straight the fretboard is. Unnotched straightedges are used to determine how level the frets are. (Photos by Skip Anderson)

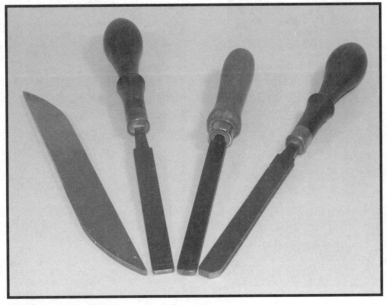

FIGURE 8.4 Recrowning files come in several sizes, shapes and cutting rasps. The half-round, dual-sized fret files work great. It is recommended to have both medium-cut and fine-cut fret files in small and medium sizes. (Photo by Skip Anderson)

Self adhesive sandpaper is perfect for any fret-leveling bar. Use 220-grit for grinding the frets to level and 1500-grit for the final burnishing and polishing.

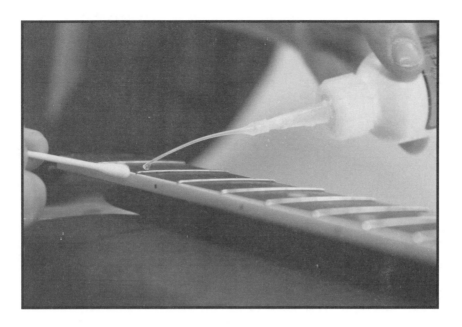

FIGURE 8.5 Super Glue® can be used to seal down a loose fret. It's a good idea to use Super Glue® to keep fret ends from popping up when the weather changes. Q-tips® are absolutely necessary when you use Super Glue®. They help to quickly absorb excess glue. (Photo by Skip Anderson)

FIGURE 8.6 Fretting hammers are needed to reseat popped up fret ends and for stubborn frets that won't seat in the middle. (Photo by Skip Anderson)

FIGURE 8.7 Flush-cut dykes (large) are used to cut the excess fret ends off after replacing a fret. (Photo by Skip Anderson)

FIGURE 8.8 Flush-cut dykes (Small) are used to remove a fret from the fretboard. (Photo by Skip Anderson)

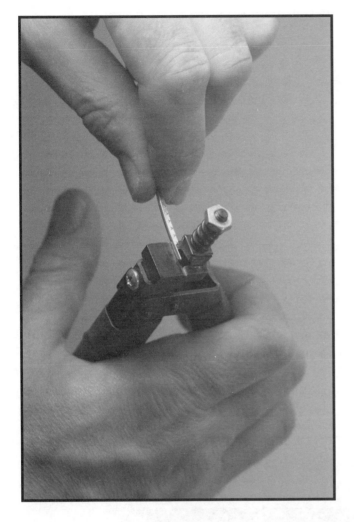

FIGURE 8.9 Fret tang nippers will remove a small piece of the fret tang in order to lay the top of the fret over the binding. (Photo by Skip Anderson)

FIGURE 8.10 A soldering iron is needed to heat up the fret to prevent the fretboard from chipping around the fretwire while it is being removed. (Photo by Skip Anderson)

A drill press vise is handy for doing fretwork on a guitar with a bolt-on neck. It is recommended to use thin strips of leather on the inside jaws of the vice. This will prevent any finish damage or marring of the wood.

Bench covers prevent the body of the guitar from getting scratched. Leather or short nap carpeting works well. Always vacuum off your bench before and after each procedure. This will minimize the risks of finish damage.

FIGURE 8.11 A brass wire brush is essential to keeping your recrowning file clean. Use it to clean out any fret debris after a few passes on the fret. (Photo by John LeVan)

Good lighting is self-explanatory. You can't see detail if you don't have good lighting. A swing-arm lamp with a magnifier is recommended for any detail work.

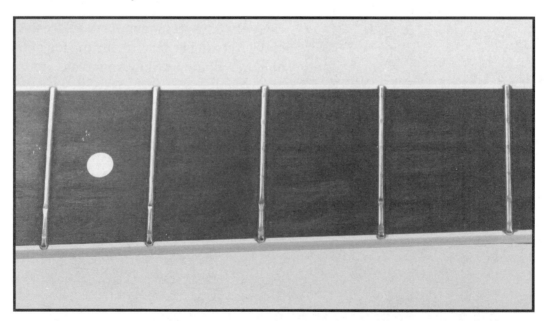

FIGURE 8.12 Frets and fretwire. Frets are made from brass, nickel, zinc and silver. Brass frets are not used very often, while frets made from nickel, zinc and silver are. Frets come in many different sizes. You can tell that its time to level them when they become dented or pitted. These ailments will cause string rattle, intonation problems and dead or choking notes. (Photo by Skip Anderson)

**Good tools and materials will help you to work
accurately, efficiently and effectively.**

Fret Leveling and Recrowning

Fretwork is a skill that takes time to develop. The most important part of this skill is your eyesight and knowing what you are looking for. Like an artist, you have to train your eyes to see things that most people ignore. To do fretwork, you need to train your eyes to see certain reflections that appear on the frets during the course of leveling and recrowning them. With good lighting and attention to detail, you will develop this skill over time. I prefer the steel bar and buckshot method for leveling frets.

Here is the procedure to level the frets on an acoustic or a guitar with a set-in neck:
1. Remove the string nut.
2. Place the neck onto the bag of buckshot (with trough), making sure that it is secure.
3. Seal frets down with Super Glue® (Skip if fretboard is maple, they're usually already sealed).
4. Measuring with a straightedge, adjust the neck until it is perfectly flat.
5. Place the leveling bar onto the frets (with the 220 grit paper down) and make a few short passes. Make sure that you pass over all of the frets.
6. Remove the leveling bar and look for the reflections on the frets to see if all the frets were scuffed equally.
7. If the frets are all scuffed equally, continue leveling until all the dents and pits are removed from the frets. If not, readjust the neck and try another pass.

Here is the procedure to level the frets on an electric guitar with a bolt-on neck:
1. Remove the string nut.
2. Remove the neck from the body.
3. Place the heel of the neck into drill press vise (make sure that there are leather guards on the jaws of your vise).
4. Set the neck onto your bag of buckshot.
5. Seal frets with Super Glue® (skip if fretboard is maple because they are already sealed in lacquer).
6. Measuring with a straightedge, adjust the neck until it is perfectly straight.
7. Place the leveling bar onto the frets (with the 220 grit paper down) and make a few short passes.
8. Remove leveling bar and look for the reflections on the frets to see if all the frets were scuffed equally.
9. If frets are all scuffed equally, continue leveling until all the dents and pits are removed from the frets. If not, readjust the neck and try another pass.

Each of these steps will be explained in detail throughout this chapter. You should only do a few passes at a time just in case the neck isn't straight, that way you'll be able to readjust the neck before you remove too much material from the frets. It is also recommended to seal the frets down with a thin solution of Super Glue® before you start. This is primarily done on rosewood or ebony fretboards. Maple fretboards are generally covered with lacquer, which usually seals them. Here is a detailed explanation of how to level the frets on an acoustic or set-in neck guitar.

1.	To remove the string nut, simply tap the front of it with a flathead screwdriver to loosen it. Then gently pull it out. Sometimes you have to slide it out sideways, other times you can pull it out from the top. If it doesn't want to budge, use a drop or two of Super Glue® solvent on the front of the nut. Always be cautious when working with solvent. Solvent can melt the finish on a guitar.

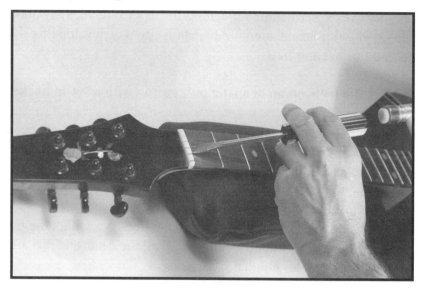

FIGURE 8.13 Be careful not to break or chip the string nut. If you do, it will have to be replaced. (Photo by Skip Anderson)

2.	When placing the neck onto the bag of buckshot, be sure that the bag in secured into the trough as we discussed earlier. Then make sure that the body of the guitar is supported so that the neck doesn't rock back and forth when sitting on top of the buckshot. This can be accomplished by using various pieces of carpet or leather as a platform under the body. It's also a good idea to lay a piece of leather, cardboard or even plastic over the top of the guitar to protect it from a slip of the file or leveling bar. It's important to keep the body and neck of the guitar steady. The use of leather to steady the guitar will also keep the neck from flexing.

3.	Next, seal the frets down (you may have to tap them down if they are unseated). If the frets pop up or are unseated, you will take off more fret material than needed when you level them. This will result in the premature replacement of the frets later on. Using your bottle of ultra-thin Super Glue®, run a thin line of glue the length of the fret. Be sure not to let the glue run over the sides of the neck, this can be vary difficult to remove. Immediately soak up any excess glue with a Q-Tip® swab.

FIGURE 8.14 The ultra-thin Super Glue® will be absorbed into the wood and help hold the fret to the fretboard. This will prevent the fret from popping up again. (Photo by Skip Anderson)

4.   With a straightedge, check to see if the neck is straight. Keep in mind that the frets are not always level with the fretboard, this is why they need to be leveled. Either the board and/or the frets could be uneven or unlevel. If you want to check the fretboard for level, use a notched straightedge. To check the frets, use a regular or unnotched straightedge. Adjust the neck until it is level or straight. If it is back-bowed, loosen the trussrod. If the neck has too much forebow, then tighten the trussrod until the neck is straight.

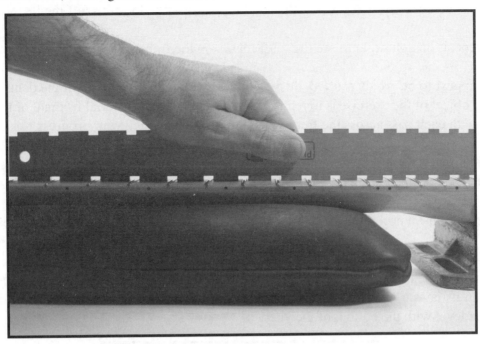

FIGURE 8.15 The notched straightedge is the most important of the two. It is the notched straightedge that will reveal the truth of the condition of the fretboard. (Photo by Skip Anderson)

5.   Place your leveling bar on top of the frets with the 220-grit sandpaper facing down (onto the frets). Make a few passes running the length of the neck (perpendicular to the frets). Be careful so that you don't slip and hit the top or the headstock of the guitar. Use short, controlled strokes with each pass. Be sure not to press down on the bar, just gently guide it across the frets.

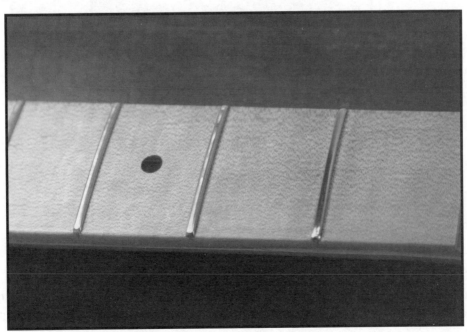

FIGURE 8.16 If the frets are not evenly scuffed after a few passes, you may have to readjust the neck to compensate for the weight of the leveling bar. (Photo by Skip Anderson)

6.   Remove the bar and inspect the frets. What you want to see are scuffmarks across all the frets, evenly. Use as much light as possible on the neck so that you can see the scuffmarks clearly. A swing-arm lamp with a florescent bulb works great. The trick is to train your eye to see the reflections of the scuffmarks on the frets. Keep in mind that many guitars will have a drop-off area on the fretboard toward the last several frets. This area is only a concern if the guitar has a cutaway. If the guitar has a cutaway, these frets need to be level with the rest of the frets. If the guitar has no cutaway, don't worry, the leveling bar usually doesn't scuff the last several frets.

You may need to reposition your light to see the scuff marks on the frets.

7.   If the frets appear to be evenly scuffed, then continue leveling them until all of the dents and pits are gone. Remember that the object of the exercise is to remove the least amount of material from all of the frets. Use short, consistent strokes with each pass across the frets. Check regularly to gauge your progress.

Removing too much material from the top of the frets will shorten the life of the frets. In other words, you will have to replace them sooner then normal.

To level the frets on a bolt-on neck, you use the same procedure with the addition of a few steps.

•   Remove the neck from the body of the guitar.
•   Place the heel of the neck into the drill press vise. Make sure that the vise has some type of padding (like leather or carpet) on its jaws to prevent it from marring or scratching the wood on the heel of the neck. The heel of the neck must be level with the bottom of the vise.

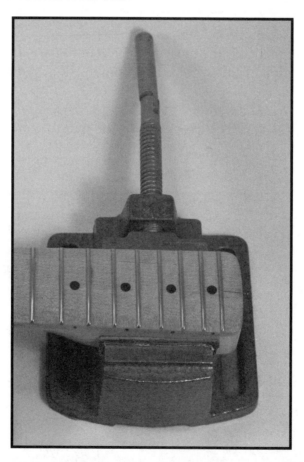

FIGURE 8.17 This vise is a great way to work on a neck without the risk of damaging the body of the guitar. However, the jaws of the vise can permanently damage the heel of a guitar neck. (Photo by Skip Anderson)

When all the frets are level, then you're ready to recrown them.

Recrowning

Recrowning the frets is a very important procedure that requires accuracy, strength and patience. Like any skill, the more you do it the better you get. For this procedure you'll need your leveling bar with 1,500-grit, self-adhesive sandpaper, one or two recrowning files, a bag of buckshot and good lighting. The object of the exercise is to round the top of the fret and remove the scuffmarks from it. Here we go.

1. Position your light so that you can clearly see the "scuffmarks" on the frets.
2. Using the recrowning file that best fits the frets, run it over the top of the frets until you cannot see the "scuff marks" on the frets.
3. Clean your recrowning file after a few passes over the fret to clean out any fret debris on the file.
4. After all of the frets are recrowned, run the leveling bar over them again, this time using the 1500-grit sandpaper. If all of the frets have thin scuff marks, then move on to step #5
5. Run the leveling bar again (with 1500- grit side), this time in the same direction as the frets (perpendicular to the neck).
6. Gently scrape the fretboard with a razor blade (unless the fretboard is lacquered or finished) to remove any tool marks from the fretboard.
7. Polish the fretboard and frets with 0000 steel wool, then vacuum off excess.
8. Apply lemon oil to the fretboard and wipe off excess.

Why is it important to recrown frets? Because flat frets can cause intonation problems, string rattle and make the guitar look substandard. That's why it's better to have a tight crown than a flathead! Here is a complete analysis of the procedures to recrown frets.

1. Correctly positioning your light will make a big difference when you need to see how the crown looks. To position your light, move it above the neck until you can see the scuffmarks. If the light isn't positioned so that you can clearly see the scuffmarks on the top of the frets, you may accidentally remove too much or too little material from the fret. This will make the fret uneven with the rest of the frets, thus causing string rattle.

FIGURE 8.18 Light is critical to this procedure. If you can't see the scuffmarks on the frets, you will not be able to properly recrown them. (Photo by Skip Anderson)

2.   Use the correct file for the job. Make sure that you choose the correct size recrowning file for the frets you are working on. There are three basic fret categories:

- Small (.074 to .085)
- Medium (.085 to .095)
- Jumbo (.095 to .120)

FIGURE 8.19 Use the fret file that is designed for the frets you are recrowning. Otherwise, you run the risk of damaging the frets. (Photo by Skip Anderson)

Recrowning files come in different categories as well:

- Small-size
- Medium-size
- Large-size
- Fine-cut
- Medium-cut
- Coarse-cut

FIGURE 8.20 The size of the fret will determine the size file you will need to use. The cut of the file refers to how fine or coarse it is. (Photo by Skip Anderson)

The number of the teeth it has determines how fine or coarse the file is. The more teeth it has, the finer the cut. I start out with a medium-cut recrowning file to remove the majority of the flat spots on the top/sides of the fret. Hold the file firmly in your dominant hand. Guide the file across the fret in single stokes and in one direction, away from yourself. If you pull the file towards you, it will drag the material you are removing across the fret and cause it to have pits and mars. Do not force the fret file across the fret; just gently guide it across the fret. Once I have removed all but a thin line of scuffmark from the top of all of the frets, I run the leveling bar over the frets with the 1500-grit sandpaper. This will help me to see if there are any high or low spots on the frets.

As with any cutting tool, you never want to force it. This will increase the chances of the file slipping off the fret and damaging the fretboard and the other frets.

If you try to force the file, here are the potential consequences:

- Slipping and damaging the fretboard.
- Slipping and damaging the frets.
- Gouging the body of the guitar.
- You could put an eye out!

Next, I use my fine-cut fret file to remove the last of the scuffmarks and to give the frets a shiny look. Again, always guide your file in one direction -away from yourself. The fine-cut file will give the fret a smooth finished look. As with the medium-cut file, let the tool do all of the work.

FIGURE 8.21 The object of the exercise is to reform the fret to have a round top and a tight crown. Notice the scuff marks on the fret on the left and the properly recrowned fret on the right.
(Photo by Skip Anderson)

Always exercise caution and use patience when performing fretwork. The fret you save could be your own. With practice you will become efficient, effective and skillful.

Gently run your leveling bar over the frets with the 1500-grit paper. Check to ensure that all of the frets are evenly scuffed and a tight crown is present. If the frets have a wide crown, repeat step 2. If the fret has a tight crown, then skip to step 5.

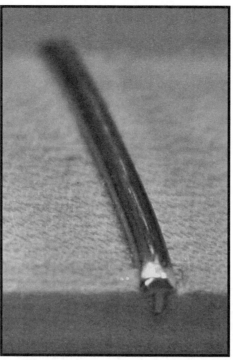

FIGURE 8.22 A thin line or scuff mark is what you're looking for. If the line is thicker than your B string, you may need to go over it with your recrowning file again. (Photo by Skip Anderson)

3.   Run you leveling bar over the frets again, but this time perpendicular to the neck. In other words, gently slide the 1500-grit side of the leveling bar in the same direction as the frets (parallel). This will remove any scuff-marks that may have been missed.

4.   Scrape the fretboard. Unless the fretboard is maple or lacquered, it's a good idea to gently scrape the fretboard with a razor blade. This will remove any tool marks. As with the fret file, let the tool do all the work. The key word is GENTLY scrape the fretboard. You don't want to leave any evidence that there were tool marks on the fretboard if you happen to have slipped while recrowning the frets. Vacuum off the fretboard.

5.   Now is the time to polish the frets with 0000 steel wool. This will give the frets a uniform look and it will also polish the fretboard. Follow the grain of the wood when you polish the fretboard. Be sure to vacuum all of the excess steel wool off the guitar and your bench.

6.   Scrub lemon oil onto the fretboard using a toothbrush. Allow the oil to be absorbed into the wood, then wipe off the excess with a paper towel. This will complete the job and help the neck to look like new.

Now you are ready to reinstall the string nut and setup the guitar. Replace the strings and follow the setup procedure detailed in first seven chapters of this book.

Partial Refretting

How many should I replace? It depends upon the condition of the fretboard and how many frets are so worn that they can't be leveled and recrowned. A partial refret is when you replace some, but not all, of the frets on a guitar. If the fretboard isn't true or level, then you are better off to do a complete refret because you'll have to plane (level and radius) the fretboard anyway. Otherwise, you will have to take off more fret material at one end of the neck than at the other when you level the frets. Unless the fretboard is in perfect condition, you should only replace up to 10 frets. Even then, you may be better off to do a complete refret because it takes almost the same amount of time.

Tools Needed:

- Fretting Hammer
- Soldering Iron
- Digital Caliper or Micrometer
- Fret Bending Tool
- Leveling Bar
- Buckshot
- Straightedges
- Sandpaper
- Q-Tips®
- Bench Cover
- Good Lighting

- Flush-Cut Dykes
- Small Pair of Flush-Cut Dykes
- Fret Tang Nippers
- X-Acto® Knife
- Fretwire
- Trough (optional)
- Recrowning Files
- Super Glue®
- Drill Press Vise
- Brass Wire Brush

1.   Measure the width and height of the frets. This is best done using a digital caliper or micrometer. It's very important to use the correct size fretwire. If you use fretwire that is too short, you'll take too much fret material off of the frets. If the fretwire is too tall, it can take longer to level and recrown the frets than if you had done a complete refret. Always use the same width fretwire as the original fretwire on the guitar. Otherwise, the guitar will play inconsistently. Nothing looks more amateurish that mismatched fretwire.

FIGURE 8.23 Measure the width and height of the fret and match it with the new wire. (Photo by Skip Anderson)

2.   Turn on your soldering iron. A soldering iron works great for heating up the frets so that you don't pull up any wood chips from the fretboard. I cut a small notch out of the tip of my soldering iron with a miniature round file. This will prevent the iron from slipping off the fret while it is being heated.

FIGURE 8.24 A miniature round file works great to notch the flat tip of your soldering iron. (Photo by Skip Anderson)

3.   Lemon oil the fretboard. The lemon oil will help soften up the wood while the frets are being heated, thus preventing any chips in the wood. Apply a generous amount of lemon oil around the frets you are going to replace.

4.   Heat up the fretwire with the tip of your soldering iron. Make sure you don't heat up the fret too much as you don't want to burn the fretboard. When you see the lemon oil start to bubble up around the fret, it is ready to be removed.

FIGURE 8.25 Keep the soldering iron centered on top of the fret and avoid tipping it to one side or the other. (Photo by Skip Anderson)

5.   Remove the fret with the small pair of flush-cut dykes. With the face of the dykes flush to the fretboard, gently squeeze the handles until the fret starts to peel out of the fretboard. NEVER pull on the fret as this will pull large pieces of wood out of the fretboard. Gently work the dykes across the fretboard as the fret is peeled out of the fretboard. Another mistake to avoid is gouging the fretboard with the dykes. This occurs when the dykes are not flush with the fretboard. Pay close attention to detail, you want to make your partial refret look stock.

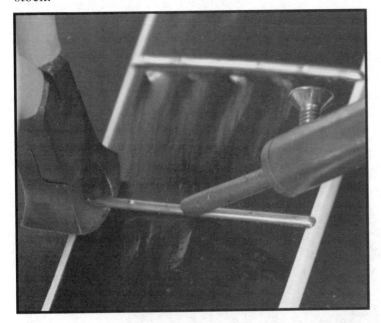

FIGURE 8.26 If you firmly place the dykes flush to the fretboard and gently squeeze them, they should force the end fret out of the slot without ripping up the wood around the fret. (Photo by Skip Anderson)

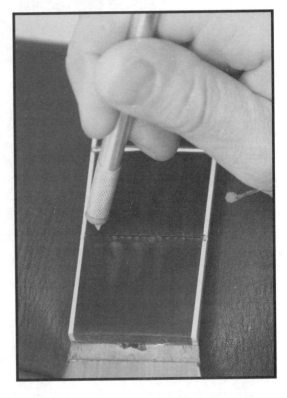

6.   Clean out the fret slot with an X-Acto® knife. Remove any wood debris and glue from the fret slot so that the new fret will go in evenly.

FIGURE 8.27 Again, do not force the knife when cleaning out the fret slots. If you slip you could gouge the fretboard, damage the binding and/or injure yourself. (Photo by Skip Anderson)

7.   Gently bend the fretwire to the radius of the fretboard. You may want to bend the wire slightly more than the radius of the fretboard so that the fret ends lie flush in the fret slot. I recommend using a fret-bending tool for this. You feed the fretwire into the bending tool and turn the crank as it bends the fretwire to the desired radius.

FIGURE 8.28 This fret-bending tool is adjustable to match the radius of any fretboard. (Photo by Skip Anderson)

8.	Cut the fretwire to the correct length. It's a good idea to leave about 1/16" extra on each side of the new fret. If the fretboard is not bound, go on to step nine. If the fretboard has binding, you will need to use a pair of fret tang nippers to remove part of the fret tang in order to lay the fret over the binding. The fret tang is the flat, barbed part on the underside of the fret. To remove part of the fret tang, place the fret (crown up) in the fret tang nipper. Then squeeze the handle to remove the tang. You only need to remove about 1/8" of the fret tang. If you measured the length of the fret correctly, this will leave about 1/8" of the fret crown (top) to lie over the binding without any tang. In other words, there will be a 1/16" gap between where the binding begins and the fret tang ends on the fret.

FIGURE 8.29 The fret can be cut longer than needed. However, it is better to cut the tang a little shorter than needed to prevent it from damaging the binding. (Photo by Skip Anderson)

9.	Tap the fret into the fretboard with the fretting hammer. This procedure requires a lot of practice. I recommend that you practice on an old neck or an inexpensive guitar before you refret an expensive one. Place the fret into the fret slot and gently tap it into the fretboard starting with the outside ends first. Work your way toward the middle, alternating between the bass and treble side of the fretboard. If you tap too hard, you can dent the fret and it will not lie flush against the fretboard. The goal is to tap the fret perfectly flush with the fretboard.

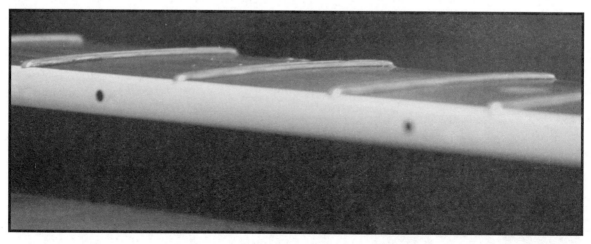

FIGURE 8.30 The goal is to install the fret flush to the fretboard, matching its radius. Be careful not to dent or deform it or the fretboard. (Photo by Skip Anderson)

10.   Seal the fret down with Super Glue®. Run a thin bead of ultra-thin Super Glue® along the length of the fret. Be careful not to drip it over the edge of the fret so that it doesn't run onto the finish of the neck. Then quickly absorb any excess with a Q-Tip®.

11.   Cut the fret ends flush with the fretboard. Use your large flush-cut dykes to cut the fret end off where it meets the edge of the fretboard. Pay careful attention to the edge of the neck so that you don't gouge it with the dykes.

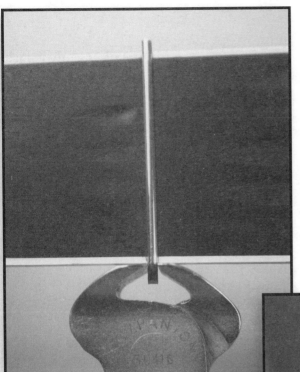

FIGURE 8.31 If the neck has binding, take special care not to gouge it. If the neck is unbound, take special care not to gouge the lacquer or the wood along the side of the fretboard. (Photo by Skip Anderson)

12.   File the fret ends with a small flat file. The fret ends should be at a 45° angle to the fretboard. You may want to run a piece of 400-grit sandpaper over the fret ends to remove any sharp edges.

FIGURE 8.32 The goal is to create an even 45° bevel on the frets along the fretboard. The fret ends should be flush to the fretboard or binding. (Photo by Skip Anderson)

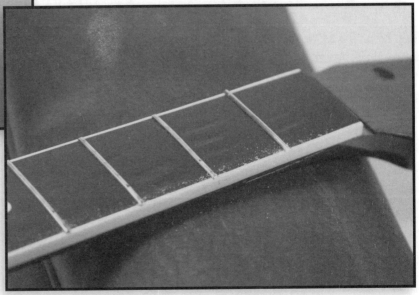

Now is the time to level and recrown the frets to complete the partial refret. Follow the procedure outlined earlier in this chapter.

Burnishing the Edges

After you have leveled and recrowned the frets, a nice finishing touch is to burnish the edges. "Burnishing" is just a fancy word for "polishing". In this case it also means smoothing the sharp edges and polishing the fret ends. You will need the following tools and materials:

- Three-Corner Miniature File
- 400-Grit Sandpaper
- 1500-Grit Sandpaper
- 0000 Steel Wool

We start with a three-corner miniature file. Gently guide the file, with one edge flat against the side of the fret, around the fret's end. Repeat this procedure on both sides of each fret end. Like all fretwork, this will require practice and patience. One or two strokes will do. The object of the exercise is to smooth off the rough edges so that the ends don't feel sharp when you slide your hand along the neck. Take care not to remove material from the fretboard or the binding with the file.

FIGURE 8.33 Keep the file squared to the fret, and gently roll it around the end of the fret.
(Photo by John LeVan)

Next, run a piece of 400-grit sandpaper along the fret ends with your hand. Then using 1500-grit sandpaper, sand the fret ends again.

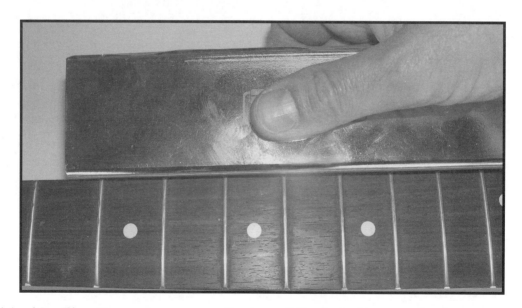

FIGURE 8.34 Avoid rolling the sandpaper over the tops of the frets; it can make them uneven. Simply skip the sandpaper along the ends of the frets. (Photo by Skip Anderson)

Now, polish the ends with 0000 steel wool and vacuum off the steel wool debris. Condition the fretboard with lemon oil. Reinstall the string nut and now you're ready to do a setup. The setup procedures are covered beginning with Chapter 3 and end with Chapter 7.

Basic Electric Guitar Wiring

There are many different types of guitars and just as many ways to wire them. In this chapter we will explore how to wire standard and custom electronic systems in everything from a basic acoustic guitar to a customized electric hot rod. Not only will we discuss how to do basic wiring, but what each component does and why it does it.

Anatomy of a Pickup

What is a pickup? A pickup is an electronic coil that transmits a signal. It transforms the vibration of the strings into an electrical signal. The pickup contains three primary parts: the magnet(s), copper wire (coil) and the bobbin. Each component plays an important role in converting the sound of the guitar strings into an electronic signal.

1.   The magnet is a ferrous material (containing iron) that can be magnetically charged and will attract other ferrous materials. Each magnet has two ends, a north end and a south end. Each end (or pole) determines the direction of the current. Magnets are usually manufactured first, then electronically charged. Some coils have flat magnets (all the same heights). Other coils have staggered magnets (various heights). The purpose of having staggered magnets is to accent certain strings. Magnetism is measured in *gauss*. There are two common methods for charging the magnets of a pickup.
   •   One method is to simply introduce the pickup to the field of another larger magnet and let it charge the magnet(s) of the pickup. The orientation, proximity and exposure time will determine the intensity and polarity of the magnet(s).
   •   Another method discharges a capacitor into a coil of wire, similar to a large solenoid. A coil of wire is wrapped around the magnet(s), the capacitor is charged with a preset amount of voltage and current, and then the capacitor is allowed to discharge into the coil. The coil will become very stable, but with a short-lived magnetic field surrounding the magnet. This short burst of magnetism can be repeated as many times as necessary to produce a consistent product.

2.   The coil is a very thin (43-42 gauge, .0022-.0025") copper wire that is coated with a nonconductive material, usually a thin plastic finish. This finish insulates the wires from each other and reduces feedback.

3.   The bobbin is the part of the pickup that the coil wire is wrapped around. Bobbins are generally made of plastic.

Each pickup coil has two ends. One end is the *start*, the other end is the *finish* of the pickup coil. The start is often the "hot" or "primary lead." The *finish* is often the "ground" or "secondary lead." There are several ways to configure pickup coils.

As a single-coil pickup.

A single-coil pickup is usually found in Strat® and Tele®-style guitars. They produce a sound that is described as a hum. A single-coil can be configured with two or even three leads. The sound is determined by how the coil is wired. Single-coil pickups have a traditional sound that can be described as everything from piercing to throaty to glassy. Each lead has a specific purpose. Most single-coil pickups have two leads (wires) attached to them. Occasionally, they are made with three leads. The extra lead is a "tap" wire. The purpose of a tap is to reduce the volume of the pickup. The tap is generally wired to a switch that cuts the volume of the pickup when the switch is engaged.

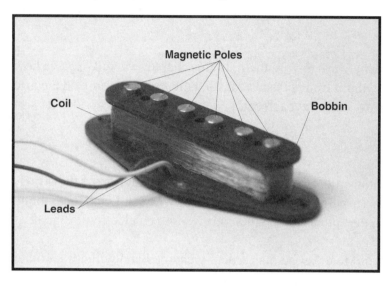

FIGURE 9.1 Diagram of a single-coil pickup. (Photo by Skip Anderson)

As a Humbucker® pickup.

The Humbucker® consists of two coils, that cancel hum. A Humbucker® pickup has two coils that are attached to each other. They are usually side-by-side, but sometimes they are stacked, with one coil on top of another. A Humbucker® can be configured with one, two, three or even four leads. Depending upon how they are wired, they can sound full and loud or much like a single coil. A Humbucker® with two leads is generally wired in a traditional manner, in its loudest and fullest configuration. With three leads, it can be "tapped," or "coil cut." That means one coil is shut off, thus creating a single coil signal. When four leads are available, there are many possibilities for wiring adventures. You can wire it in "series" traditional, "tapped," "parallel," "in phase" and "out of phase." As you can see, there are many ways to wire a Humbucker® and we will explore many of them in this chapter. Each wiring configuration will produce a different sound or tone.

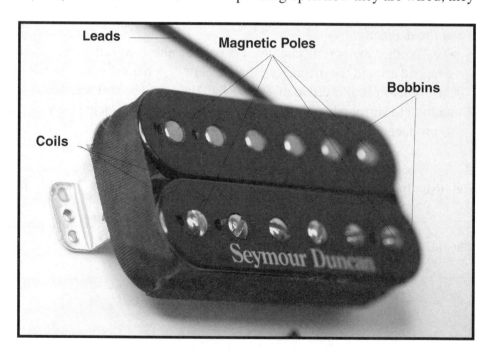

FIGURE 9.2 This is a diagram of a Humbucker® (aka double-coil) pickup. (Photo by Skip Anderson)

In Series

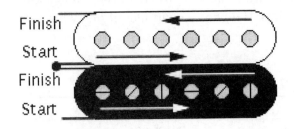

Humbucker® wired in series

Two coils are wired together in series in the following configuration; The *"finish"* of coil No. 1 is wired to the *"start"* of coil No. 2. Generally the *"start"* is the "hot" and the *"finish"* is the "ground" wire.

FIGURE 9.3 Note the direction of the current when two coils are wired in series. (Illustration by John LeVan)

In Parallel

Two coils are wired together in parallel when the *"starts"* of both coils are wired together. The *"finish"* wires are wired together as well. This configuration produces a clean, bright tone without the traditional single-coil hum. Again, in many cases, the *start* is the hot wire and the *finish* is the ground wire.

FIGURE 9.4 Note the direction of the current when two coils are wired in parallel. (Illustration by John LeVan)

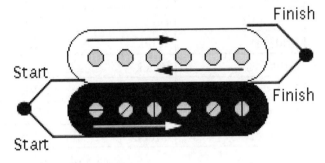

Humbucker® wired in Parallel

Phase

The term phase refers to the direction of current passing through the coil. There are two ways of defining phase as it relates to a pickup: *sonically* and *magnetically*. "Sonically" refers to the pickup having maximum volume and tone. "Magnetically" refers to the magnetic charge flowing in the same direction between two coils. Sonic phase is the format we will follow when wiring a guitar. How the coils are wired in relationship to each other will determine its *phase*. A Humbucker® wired in *phase (sonically)*, sounds full and loud the same as wired *out of phase* magnetically. Wired *out of phase (sonically)*, it will sound bright, thin and great for funk or punk rock, the same as it would if wired *in phase* magnetically.

Polarity

Polarity refers to the relationship between positive and negative electrical currents; in other words, the direction the electrical currents travel (north/south) through a circuit.

Color Codes

Color Codes are used to identify the purpose of each wire found in a wiring harness. Many of the humbucking pickups have four conductors (wires) plus a braided shield (ground wire). Below is a chart identifying what each color means in regards to its manufacturer.

Color codes for the various brands of four-conductor pickups

Brand	A (start)	B (finish)	C (start)	D (finish)
Anderson®	Red	Green	Black	White
Kent Armstrong®	Green/Black	White	Red	Blue
Benedetto®	Red	Black	Green	White
DiMarzio®	Red	Black	Green	White
Duncan®	Black	White	Green	Red
Fralin®	White	Red	Black	Red
Gibson®	Black	Green	Red	White
Jackson®	Green	White	Black	Red
Lawrence®	Black	Green	Red	White
Schaller®	Green	White	Yellow	Brown

Legend provided by Stewart-MacDonald® *Trade Secrets Vol. 8*

Legend

The legend below illustrates the different combinations available with each manufacturer's color codes.

Legend for different wiring combinations

Series Linked In Phase	A = Hot	B & D = Series Link	C = Ground
Series Linked Out of Phase	A = Hot	B & C = Series Link	D= Ground
Parallel Linked In Phase	A & D = Hot	B & C = Ground	
Parallel Linked Out of Phase	A & C = Hot	B & D = Ground	

Legend provided by Stewart-MacDonald® *Trade Secrets Vol. 8*

(Bare/shield wires are always soldered to a ground.
"Phase" is in reference to "sonic phase", not "magnetic phase")

Most single-coils have only two leads, one hot, and the other a ground. The colors vary, so it is difficult to know them all. Experiment with wiring them to find the best sound. If you wire it backwards, it won't damage the coil. If nothing else, you have a 50/50 chance of getting it right the first time. Alligator clips are very useful for hooking up the pickups without soldering the leads. It speeds up the process of elimination and helps you to avoid over soldering the other components.

RW/RP, LFTW and Other Acronyms

RW/RP-This acronym translates to reverse wound, reverse polarity

In other words, the coil is wound in the opposite direction of a standard pickup coil. This arrangement is very useful when you run two pickup coils at the same time. When one of the coils is RW/RP and the other is wound standard, it creates a Humbucker® when both are in use at the same time. This eliminates the extra noise produced by each single-coil pickup. In most cases, the second-coil in a Humbucker® is reverse-wound or RW/RP. In a Strat®-style guitar, the middle pickup should be RW/RP so that the coils hum-cancel when the switch is in the second or fourth position. Tele®-style guitars sound best when the neck pickup is RW/RP because when the selector switch is in the middle position...*you guessed it*...the pickups will hum-cancel (become a Humbucker®). RW/RP pickup coils are useful when wiring different combinations of double and single-coil pickups. These combinations will be explored later in this chapter.

LFT/W-This acronym refers to a left-wound or left-handed coil.

This primarily applies to either a vintage Stratocaster® or a left-handed guitar with staggered poles (magnets). Some guitars have been routed in a way that requires LFT/W coils in order to use staggered pole pickups as they were designed.

SPST

Single-pole, single-throw. These terms describe a type of switch with one row of three lugs, the center lug being the output. The switch can be used as an:

1. On/On
    • Coil Tap/Series
2. On/Off
    • Coil Tap/Off
    • Series/Off

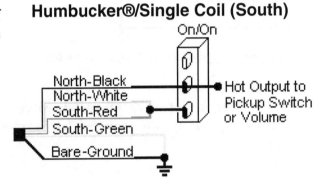

FIGURE 9.5 Diagram of a SPST switch wired as a series coil tap. (Diagram provided by Seymour Duncan®)

DPDT

Double-pole, double-throw. These switches usually have six terminals (two rows of three). The two in the middle are generally output lugs. They are available as a toggle, push/pull or push/push switch. Used for many different wiring configurations, the DPDT is great for expanding the abilities of your pickups. The different configurations include:

1. On/On
    • Coil Tap/Series
    • In Phase/Out of Phase
    • Series/Parallel

2. On/Off/On
    • Coil Tap/Off/Series

3. On/On/On
    • Coil Tap/Series/Parallel

Ohms (Ω) are the standard unit of measure for electrical resistance.

Humbucker/Single Coil(S)/Out of Phase

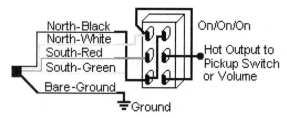

North-Black
North-White
South-Red
South-Green
Bare-Ground

On/On/On

Hot Output to
Pickup Switch
or Volume

Ground

Humbucker/Out of Phase-use an On/On switch
Humbucker/OFF/Out Phase-use an On/Off/On switch

FIGURE 9.7 Diagram of a DPDT switch wired Coil Tap/Series. (Diagram provided by Seymour Duncan®)

Series/Parallel

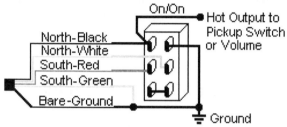

On/On

Hot Output to
Pickup Switch
or Volume

North-Black
North-White
South-Red
South-Green
Bare-Ground

Ground

For Series/OFF/Parallel-Use an On/Off/On switch

FIGURE 9.9 Diagram of a DPDT switch wired Series/Off/ Coil Tap. (Diagram provided by Seymour Duncan®)

Humbucker/OFF/Single Coil (South)

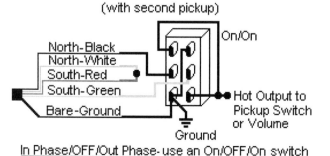

North-Black
North-White
South-Red
South-Green
Bare-Ground

On/Off/On

Hot Output to
Pickup Switch
or Volume

Ground

FIGURE 9.11 Diagram of a DPDT switch wired Series/ Coil Tap /Parallel. (Diagram provided by Seymour Duncan®)

In Phase/Out of Phase
(with second pickup)

North-Black
North-White
South-Red
South-Green
Bare-Ground

On/On

Hot Output to
Pickup Switch
or Volume

Ground

In Phase/OFF/Out Phase-use an On/OFF/On switch

FIGURE 9.6 Diagram of a DPDT switch wired Series/Coil Tap/Out of Phase. (Diagram provided by Seymour Duncan®)

Humbucker /Single Coil (North)

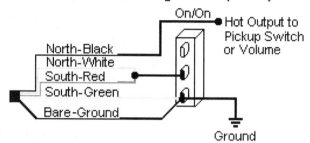

On/On

Hot Output to
Pickup Switch
or Volume

North-Black
North-White
South-Red
South-Green
Bare-Ground

Ground

FIGURE 9.8 Diagram of a DPDT switch wired Series/ Parallel. (Diagram provided by Seymour Duncan®)

Humbucker/OFF/Single Coil (North)

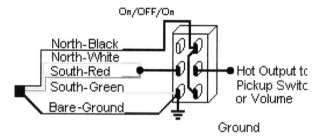

On/OFF/On

North-Black
North-White
South-Red
South-Green
Bare-Ground

Hot Output to
Pickup Switch
or Volume

Ground

FIGURE 9.10 Diagram of a DPDT switch wired Series/Off/ Coil Tap. (Diagram provided by Seymour Duncan®)

Humbucker/Single Coil(S)/Parallel

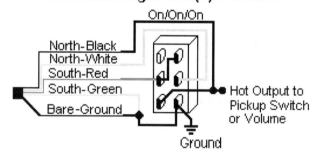

On/On/On

North-Black
North-White
South-Red
South-Green
Bare-Ground

Hot Output to
Pickup Switch
or Volume

Ground

FIGURE 9.12 Diagram of a DPDT switch wired In Phase/Out of Phase. (Diagram provided by Seymour Duncan®)

Volume Potentiometer

A volume "pot" controls the volume or loudness of a pickup or group of pickups. They are most commonly used in two values, 250KΩ and 500KΩ, where K=thousands and Ω=Ohms. 250KΩ pots are normally used with single-coil pickups because they are "sweeter" or "less bright" sounding. 500KΩ pots are better for humbucking because they are brighter sounding than the 250KΩ pots.

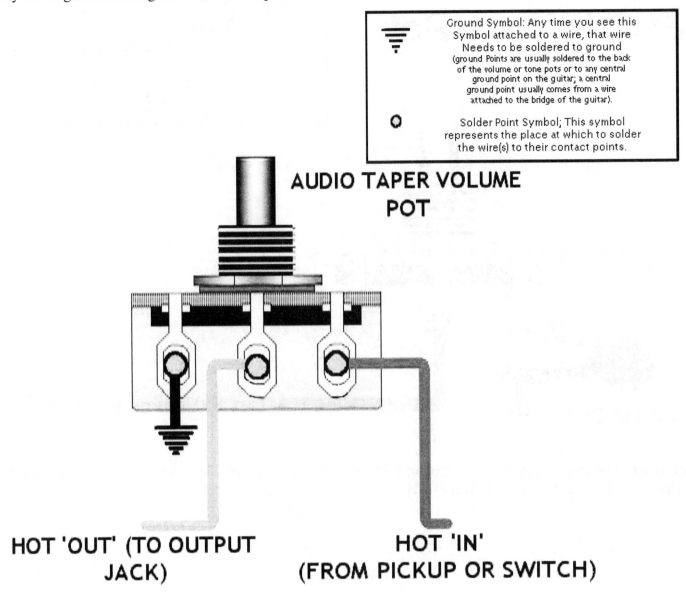

FIGURE 9.13 Volume pots have three lugs: input, output and ground. (Diagram provided by Seymour Duncan®)

Tone Potentiometer

Tone pots roll off the brightness or treble of the pickups. Tone pots can be wired to control one or many pickups at the same time; 250KΩ pots are the standard for tone controls.

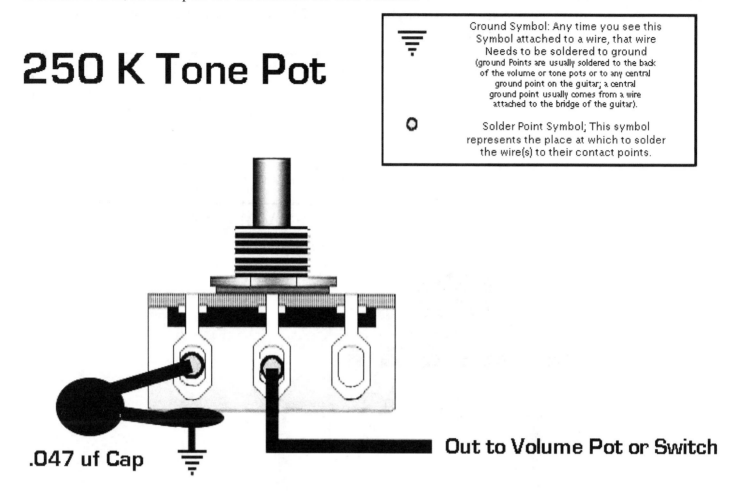

FIGURE 9.14 Tone pots also have three lugs: input, output and ground, but can be wired in several ways. (Diagram provided by Seymour Duncan®)

Three-Way Switch

A three-way switch is generally used in a guitar with two pickups. They are also found in a lot of vintage Stratocaster® guitars. "Three-way" refers to the ability to turn on either or both pickups. The configuration is as follows.

Position #:
1.   Bridge Pickup
2.   Bridge/Neck Pickups
3.   Neck Pickup

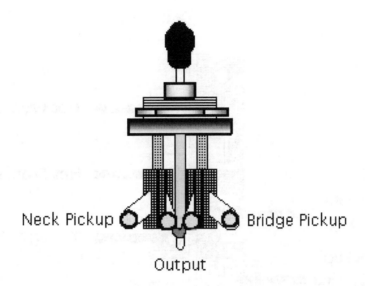

FIGURE 9.15 Three-way switch diagram. (Diagram provided by Seymour Duncan®)

Four-Way Switch

The four-way switch will add an extra tone quality to a two-pickup guitar. The configuration is as follows.
Position #:

1.   Bridge Pickup Only
2.   Bridge/Neck in Series
3.   Bridge/Neck in Parallel
4.   Neck Pickup Only

4-Way Lever Switch

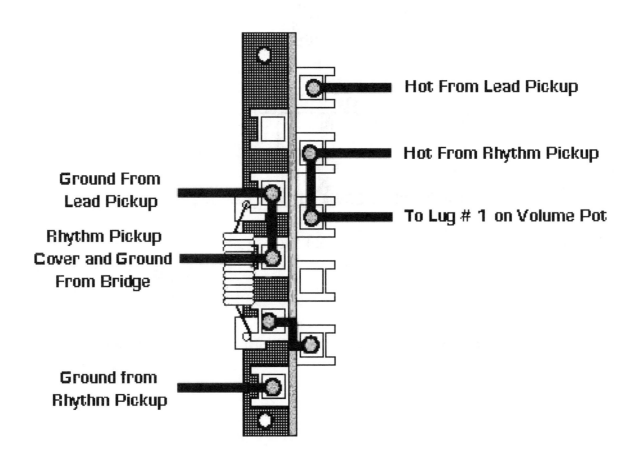

FIGURE 9.16 Four-way switch diagram. (diagram provided by Seymour Duncan®)

Five-Way Switch

The five-way switch is more commonly found in guitars with three pickups. It allows you to turn on just one of the pickups, or a combination of pickups. You can also wire the tone pots to the switch and control them as per the position of the switch. In other words, you can wire the lower tone pot to be active only when the five-way switch is in the fourth and fifth positions. We will explore other options later in this chapter. The configuration is as follows.

Position #:
1. Bridge Pickup Only
2. Bridge/Middle Pickups
3. Middle Pickup Only
4. Middle/Neck Pickups
5. Neck Pickup Only

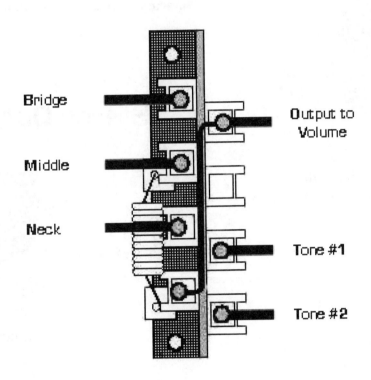

FIGURE 9.17 Five-way switch diagram. (diagram provided by Seymour Duncan®)

Output Jacks

There are many varieties of output jacks; mono, stereo, TRS (tip, ring, sleeve), endpin and flush-mount are the more common types. Each one has a specific purpose.

1. Mono jacks are found on:
    • Most electric guitars with passive pickups.
    • Acoustic guitars with passive pickups.
2. Stereo jacks are found on:
    • Electric guitars with active pickups.
    • Acoustic guitars with active pickups.
    • Acoustic guitars with passive pickup plus a microphone.
3. TRS (tip, ring, sleeve) jacks are found on:
    • Acoustic guitar with an active pickup/microphone combination. Used to run each electronic device (mic/pickup) to two different sources (amps/channels on a mixer).

Mono Output Jack

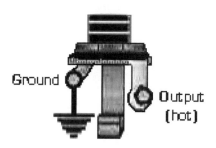

**FIGURE 9.18 Mono jack diagram.
(Diagram provided by Seymour Duncan®)**

**FIGURE 9.19 Stereo jack diagram.
(Diagram provided by Seymour Duncan®)**

Stereo Output Jack

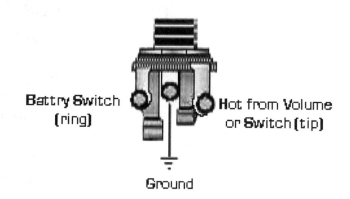

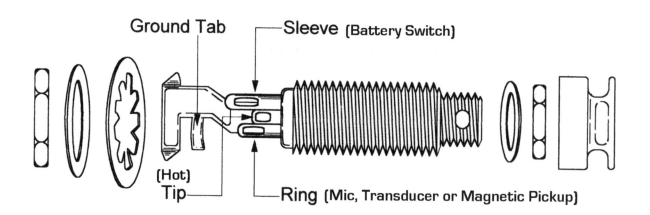

FIGURE 9.20 TRS jack diagram. (Diagram provided by Seymour Duncan®)

Active electronics generally run from a power source (like a battery) and require a special circuit in order to work as intended. They are found in acoustic guitars, electric guitars, basses and other stringed instruments.

Passive electronics are most common in electric guitars. In fact, most electric guitar pickups are passive. They do not require any special preamps or batteries in order to work. Occasionally found in acoustic instruments, passive systems usually have weak output when used in a non-magnetic medium.

Wax potting is the process of saturating a pickup coil with wax. This ensures that its components remain motionless, thus, preventing microphonic feedback. Most pickup manufacturers wax pot their pickups. One of the most effective methods of wax potting is vacuum encapsulation. Vacuum encapsulation provides excellent wax penetration and consistent results.

Soldering Tips
1. Never blow on the solder to cool it, this can produce a "cold weld" which can interfere with electrical signals.
2. Always keep your tip clean. Clean the tip of your soldering iron with a sponge or paper towel often when you wire a circuit.
3. Tin your iron. Melt a little bit of solder onto the tip of your iron before you begin. This will speed up the iron's ability to melt an old solder joint.
4. Don't oversolder. The more solder you use, the better the chance of a "cold weld." The longer you heat a component, the more you increase the potential of failure. Keep your solder joints clean, neat, and quick.

Wiring Diagrams

The following is a collection of wiring configurations of the most common electric guitars and basses.

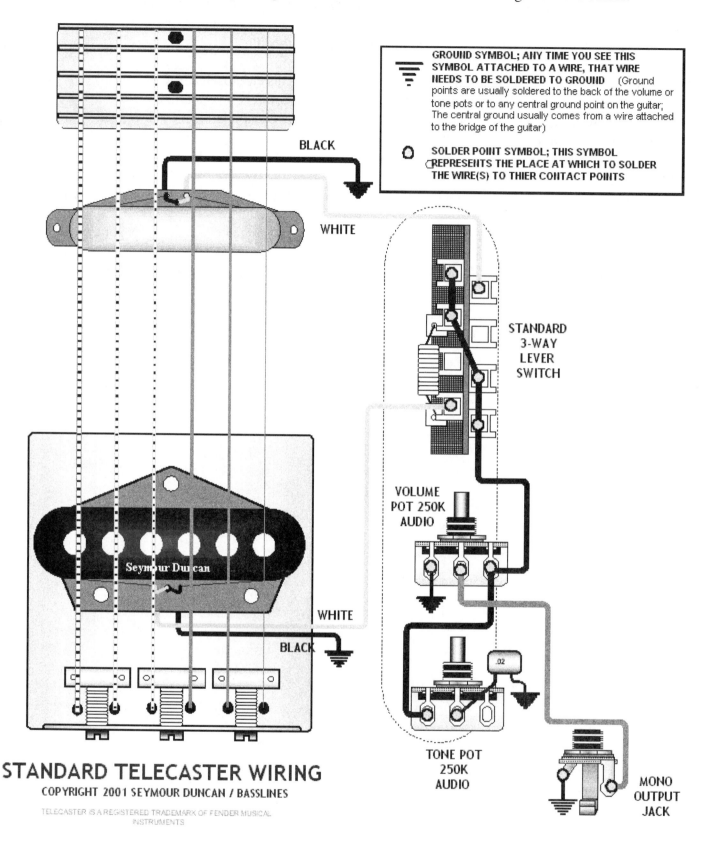

FIGURE 9.21 Telecaster®. (Diagram provided by Seymour Duncan®)

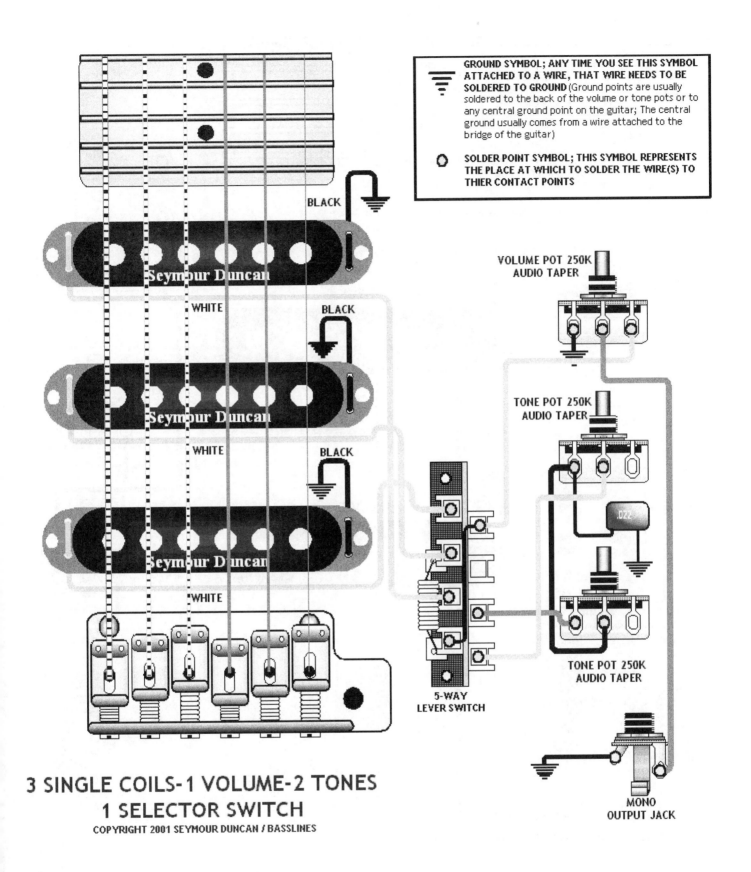

GROUND SYMBOL; ANY TIME YOU SEE THIS SYMBOL ATTACHED TO A WIRE, THAT WIRE NEEDS TO BE SOLDERED TO GROUND (Ground points are usually soldered to the back of the volume or tone pots or to any central ground point on the guitar; The central ground usually comes from a wire attached to the bridge of the guitar)

SOLDER POINT SYMBOL; THIS SYMBOL REPRESENTS THE PLACE AT WHICH TO SOLDER THE WIRE(S) TO THIER CONTACT POINTS

BLACK

VOLUME POT 250K
AUDIO TAPER

WHITE

BLACK

TONE POT 250K
AUDIO TAPER

WHITE

BLACK

.022

TONE POT 250K
AUDIO TAPER

WHITE

5-WAY
LEVER SWITCH

MONO
OUTPUT JACK

3 SINGLE COILS-1 VOLUME-2 TONES
1 SELECTOR SWITCH
COPYRIGHT 2001 SEYMOUR DUNCAN / BASSLINES

FIGURE 9.22 Stratocaster®. (Diagram provided by Seymour Duncan®)

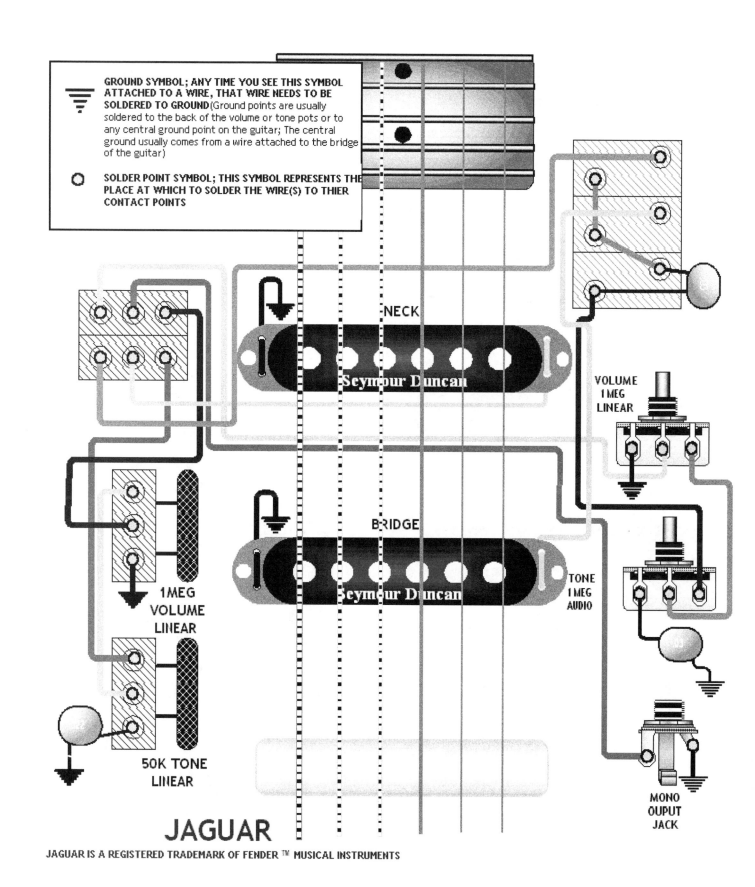

GROUND SYMBOL; ANY TIME YOU SEE THIS SYMBOL ATTACHED TO A WIRE, THAT WIRE NEEDS TO BE SOLDERED TO GROUND(Ground points are usually soldered to the back of the volume or tone pots or to any central ground point on the guitar; The central ground usually comes from a wire attached to the bridge of the guitar)

SOLDER POINT SYMBOL; THIS SYMBOL REPRESENTS THE PLACE AT WHICH TO SOLDER THE WIRE(S) TO THIER CONTACT POINTS

NECK

Seymour Duncan

BRIDGE

Seymour Duncan

1MEG VOLUME LINEAR

50K TONE LINEAR

VOLUME 1 MEG LINEAR

TONE 1 MEG AUDIO

MONO OUPUT JACK

JAGUAR

JAGUAR IS A REGISTERED TRADEMARK OF FENDER ™ MUSICAL INSTRUMENTS

FIGURE 9.23 Jaguar®. (Diagram provided by Seymour Duncan®)

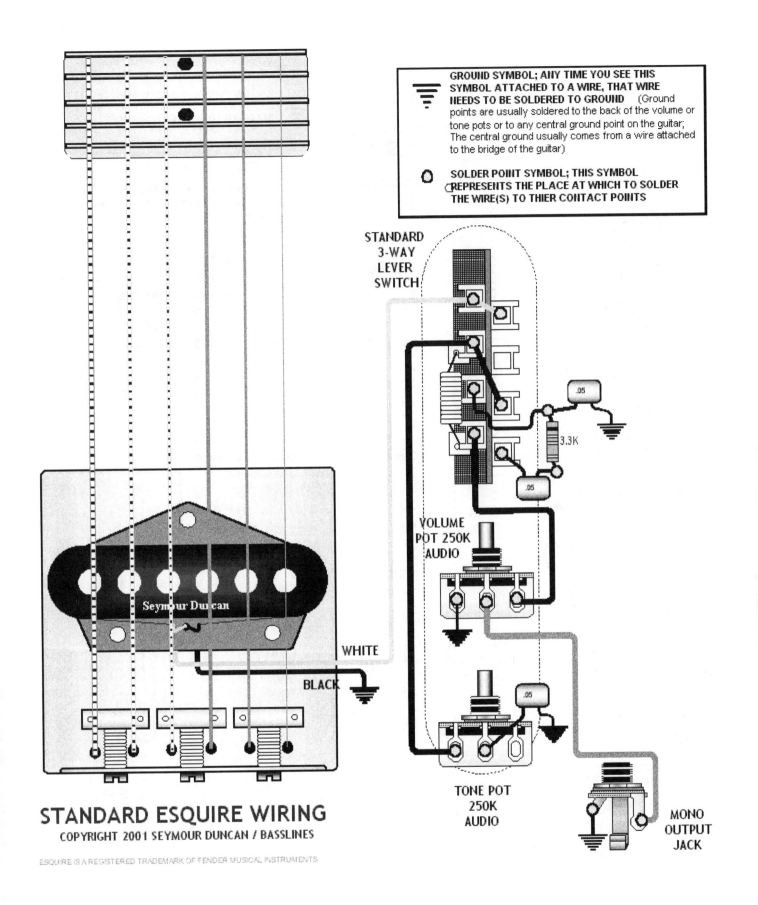

GROUND SYMBOL; ANY TIME YOU SEE THIS SYMBOL ATTACHED TO A WIRE, THAT WIRE NEEDS TO BE SOLDERED TO GROUND (Ground points are usually soldered to the back of the volume or tone pots or to any central ground point on the guitar; The central ground usually comes from a wire attached to the bridge of the guitar)

SOLDER POINT SYMBOL; THIS SYMBOL REPRESENTS THE PLACE AT WHICH TO SOLDER THE WIRE(S) TO THIER CONTACT POINTS

STANDARD 3-WAY LEVER SWITCH

.05

3.3K

.05

VOLUME POT 250K AUDIO

WHITE

BLACK

.05

TONE POT 250K AUDIO

MONO OUTPUT JACK

STANDARD ESQUIRE WIRING
COPYRIGHT 2001 SEYMOUR DUNCAN / BASSLINES

ESQUIRE IS A REGISTERED TRADEMARK OF FENDER MUSICAL INSTRUMENTS

FIGURE 9.24 Esquire®. (Diagram provided by Seymour Duncan®)

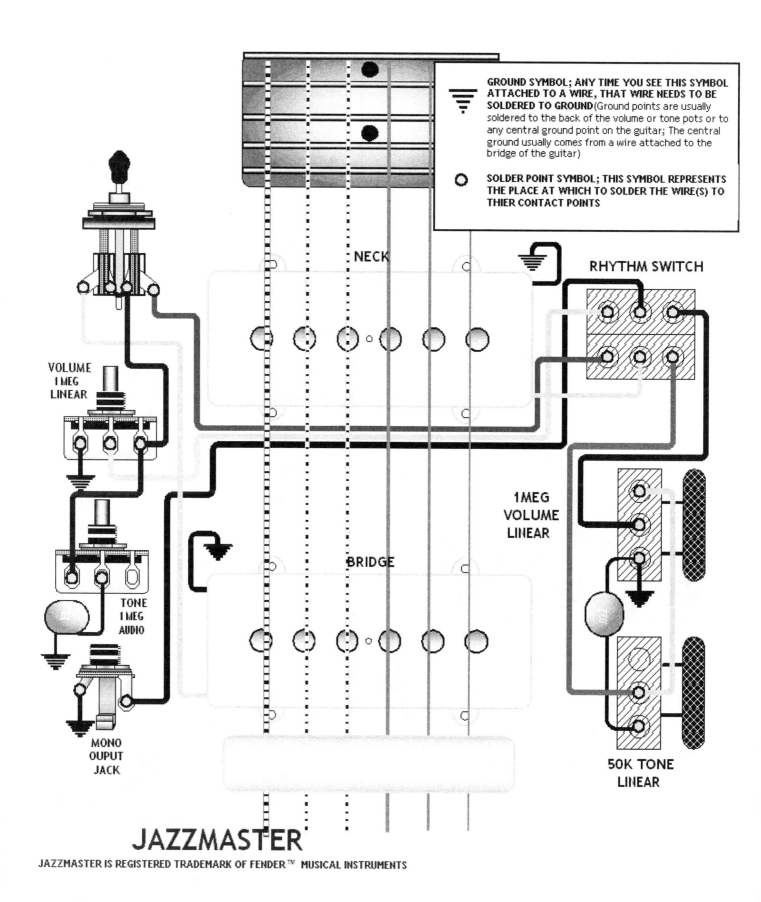

GROUND SYMBOL; ANY TIME YOU SEE THIS SYMBOL ATTACHED TO A WIRE, THAT WIRE NEEDS TO BE SOLDERED TO GROUND(Ground points are usually soldered to the back of the volume or tone pots or to any central ground point on the guitar; The central ground usually comes from a wire attached to the bridge of the guitar)

SOLDER POINT SYMBOL; THIS SYMBOL REPRESENTS THE PLACE AT WHICH TO SOLDER THE WIRE(S) TO THIER CONTACT POINTS

NECK

RHYTHM SWITCH

VOLUME
1 MEG
LINEAR

1MEG
VOLUME
LINEAR

TONE
1 MEG
AUDIO

BRIDGE

MONO
OUPUT
JACK

50K TONE
LINEAR

JAZZMASTER

JAZZMASTER IS REGISTERED TRADEMARK OF FENDER™ MUSICAL INSTRUMENTS

FIGURE 9.25 Jazzmaster®. (Diagram provided by Seymour Duncan®)

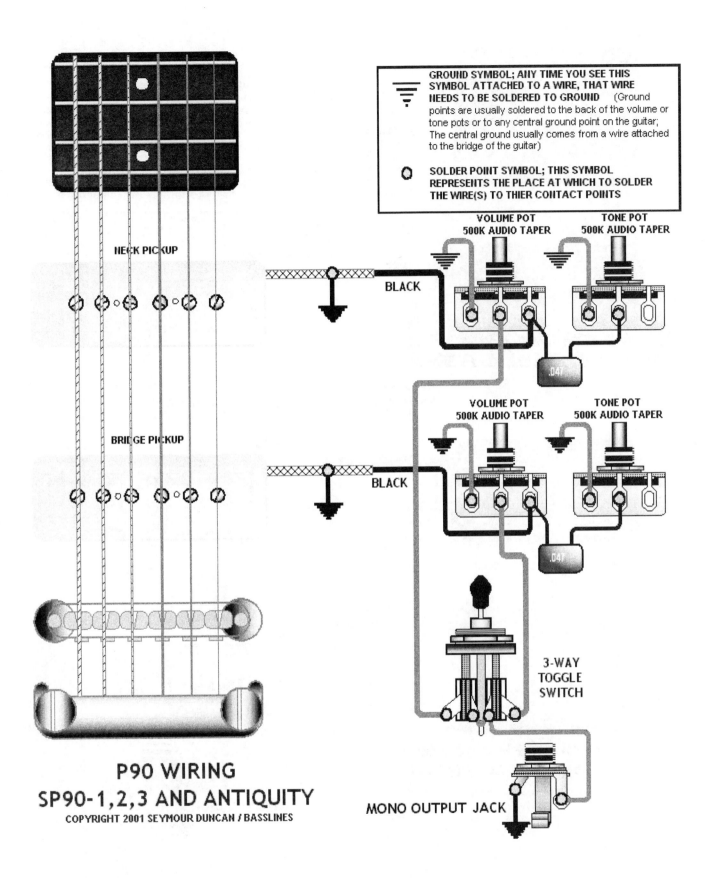

GROUND SYMBOL; ANY TIME YOU SEE THIS SYMBOL ATTACHED TO A WIRE, THAT WIRE NEEDS TO BE SOLDERED TO GROUND   (Ground points are usually soldered to the back of the volume or tone pots or to any central ground point on the guitar; The central ground usually comes from a wire attached to the bridge of the guitar)

SOLDER POINT SYMBOL; THIS SYMBOL REPRESENTS THE PLACE AT WHICH TO SOLDER THE WIRE(S) TO THIER CONTACT POINTS

NECK PICKUP

BRIDGE PICKUP

VOLUME POT 500K AUDIO TAPER

TONE POT 500K AUDIO TAPER

BLACK

.047

VOLUME POT 500K AUDIO TAPER

TONE POT 500K AUDIO TAPER

BLACK

.047

3-WAY TOGGLE SWITCH

MONO OUTPUT JACK

P90 WIRING
SP90-1,2,3 AND ANTIQUITY
COPYRIGHT 2001 SEYMOUR DUNCAN / BASSLINES

FIGURE 9.26 P-90®. (Diagram provided by Seymour Duncan®)

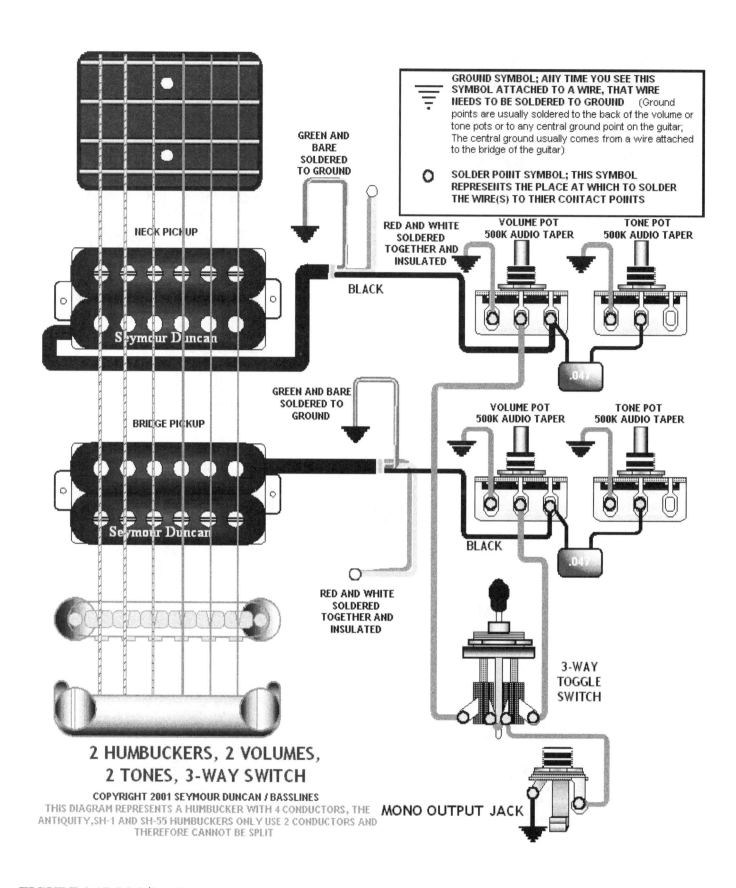

GREEN AND
BARE
SOLDERED
TO GROUND

GROUND SYMBOL; ANY TIME YOU SEE THIS
SYMBOL ATTACHED TO A WIRE, THAT WIRE
NEEDS TO BE SOLDERED TO GROUND   (Ground
points are usually soldered to the back of the volume or
tone pots or to any central ground point on the guitar;
The central ground usually comes from a wire attached
to the bridge of the guitar)

SOLDER POINT SYMBOL; THIS SYMBOL
REPRESENTS THE PLACE AT WHICH TO SOLDER
THE WIRE(S) TO THIER CONTACT POINTS

NECK PICKUP

Seymour Duncan

RED AND WHITE
SOLDERED
TOGETHER AND
INSULATED

BLACK

VOLUME POT
500K AUDIO TAPER

TONE POT
500K AUDIO TAPER

.047

GREEN AND BARE
SOLDERED TO
GROUND

BRIDGE PICKUP

Seymour Duncan

VOLUME POT
500K AUDIO TAPER

TONE POT
500K AUDIO TAPER

BLACK

.047

RED AND WHITE
SOLDERED
TOGETHER AND
INSULATED

3-WAY
TOGGLE
SWITCH

2 HUMBUCKERS, 2 VOLUMES,
2 TONES, 3-WAY SWITCH

COPYRIGHT 2001 SEYMOUR DUNCAN / BASSLINES
THIS DIAGRAM REPRESENTS A HUMBUCKER WITH 4 CONDUCTORS, THE
ANTIQUITY,SH-1 AND SH-55 HUMBUCKERS ONLY USE 2 CONDUCTORS AND
THEREFORE CANNOT BE SPLIT

MONO OUTPUT JACK

FIGURE 9.27 SG®/Les Paul®. (Diagram provided by Seymour Duncan®)

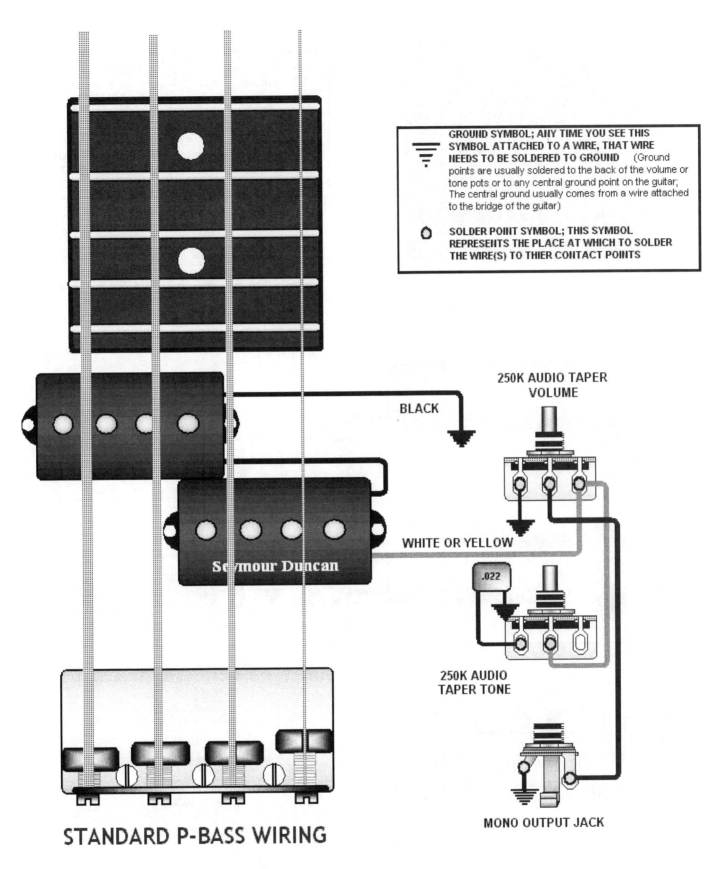

GROUND SYMBOL; ANY TIME YOU SEE THIS SYMBOL ATTACHED TO A WIRE, THAT WIRE NEEDS TO BE SOLDERED TO GROUND (Ground points are usually soldered to the back of the volume or tone pots or to any central ground point on the guitar; The central ground usually comes from a wire attached to the bridge of the guitar)

SOLDER POINT SYMBOL; THIS SYMBOL REPRESENTS THE PLACE AT WHICH TO SOLDER THE WIRE(S) TO THIER CONTACT POINTS

250K AUDIO TAPER VOLUME

BLACK

WHITE OR YELLOW

.022

250K AUDIO TAPER TONE

MONO OUTPUT JACK

Seymour Duncan

STANDARD P-BASS WIRING

PRECISION BASS IS A REGISTERED TRADEMARK OF FENDER MUSICAL INSTRUMENTS

FIGURE 9.28 P-Bass®. (Diagram provided by Seymour Duncan®)

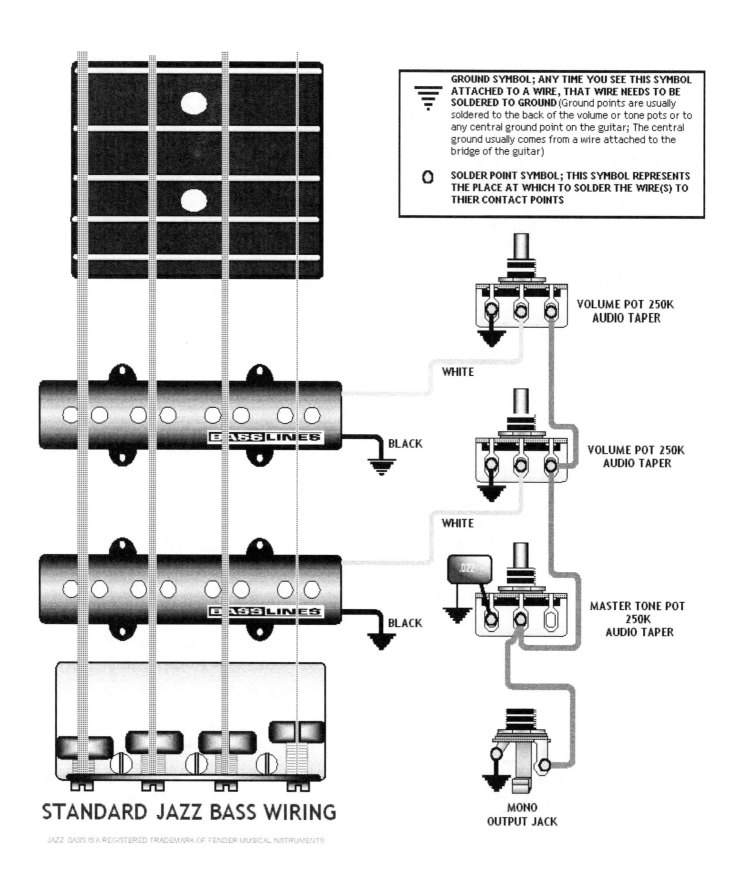

GROUND SYMBOL; ANY TIME YOU SEE THIS SYMBOL ATTACHED TO A WIRE, THAT WIRE NEEDS TO BE SOLDERED TO GROUND (Ground points are usually soldered to the back of the volume or tone pots or to any central ground point on the guitar; The central ground usually comes from a wire attached to the bridge of the guitar)

SOLDER POINT SYMBOL; THIS SYMBOL REPRESENTS THE PLACE AT WHICH TO SOLDER THE WIRE(S) TO THIER CONTACT POINTS

VOLUME POT 250K
AUDIO TAPER

WHITE

BLACK

VOLUME POT 250K
AUDIO TAPER

WHITE

BLACK

MASTER TONE POT
250K
AUDIO TAPER

MONO
OUTPUT JACK

STANDARD JAZZ BASS WIRING

JAZZ BASS IS A REGISTERED TRADEMARK OF FENDER MUSICAL INSTRUMENTS

FIGURE 9.29 Jazz Bass®. (Diagram provided by Seymour Duncan®)

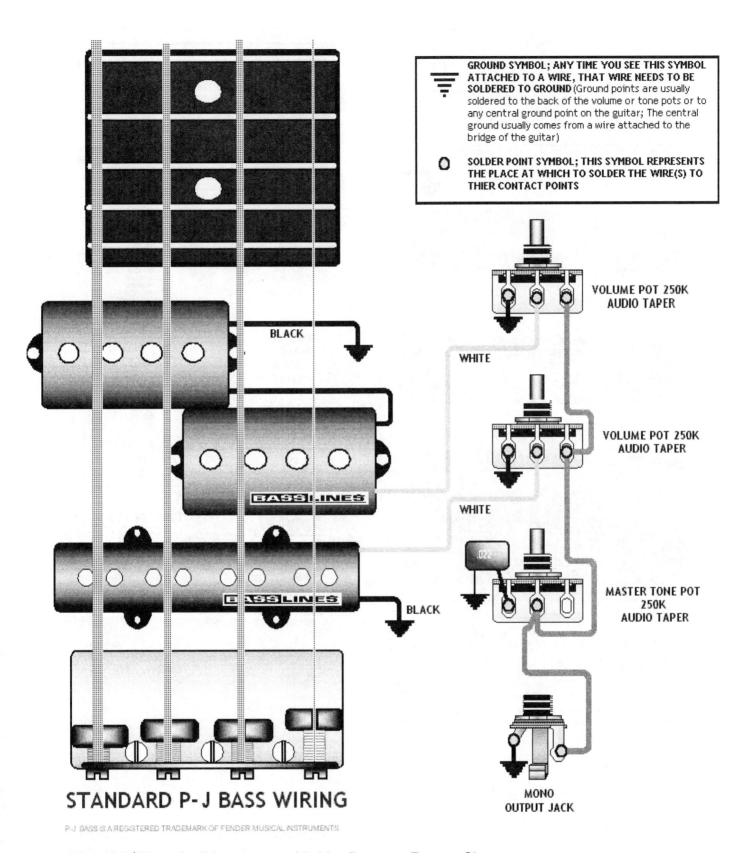

GROUND SYMBOL; ANY TIME YOU SEE THIS SYMBOL ATTACHED TO A WIRE, THAT WIRE NEEDS TO BE SOLDERED TO GROUND (Ground points are usually soldered to the back of the volume or tone pots or to any central ground point on the guitar; The central ground usually comes from a wire attached to the bridge of the guitar)

SOLDER POINT SYMBOL; THIS SYMBOL REPRESENTS THE PLACE AT WHICH TO SOLDER THE WIRE(S) TO THIER CONTACT POINTS

BLACK

WHITE

VOLUME POT 250K
AUDIO TAPER

VOLUME POT 250K
AUDIO TAPER

WHITE

.022

BLACK

MASTER TONE POT
250K
AUDIO TAPER

MONO
OUTPUT JACK

STANDARD P-J BASS WIRING

P-J BASS IS A REGISTERED TRADEMARK OF FENDER MUSICAL INSTRUMENTS

FIGURE 9.30 P/J Bass®. (Diagram provided by Seymour Duncan®)

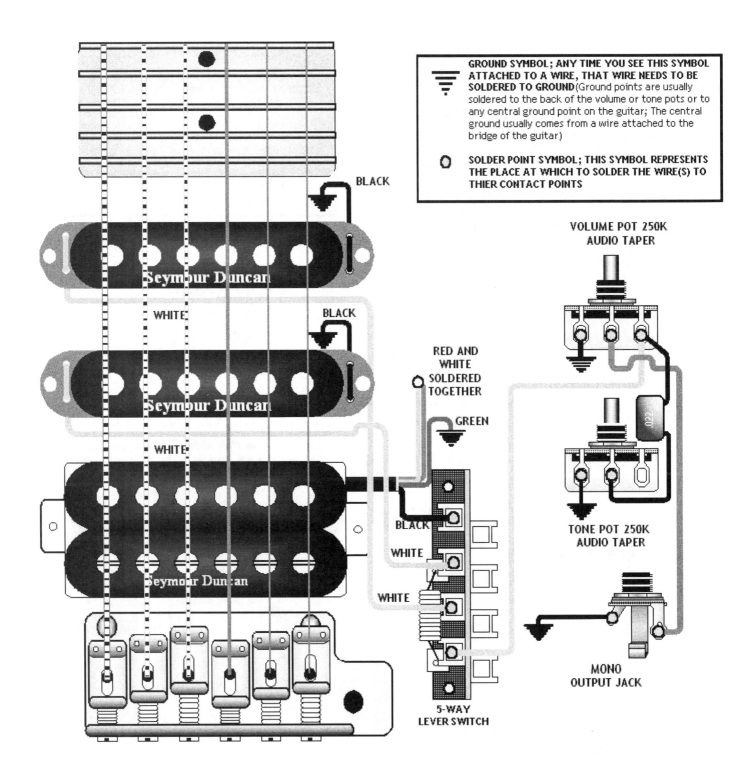

BLACK

WHITE

BLACK

WHITE

WHITE

RED AND WHITE SOLDERED TOGETHER

GREEN

BLACK

WHITE

WHITE

5-WAY LEVER SWITCH

VOLUME POT 250K AUDIO TAPER

TONE POT 250K AUDIO TAPER

MONO OUTPUT JACK

1 HUMBUCKER, 2 SINGLE COILS-1 VOLUME-1 TONE, 1 SELECTOR SWITCH

COPYRIGHT 2001 SEYMOUR DUNCAN / BASSLINES

THIS DIAGRAM SHOWS A 4-CONDUCTOR HUMBUCKER. YOU CAN USE A SINGLE CONDUCTOR HUMBUCKER SUCH AS A SH-55 SETH LOVER, SH-1 59' MODEL OR ANTIQUITY WITH THE SAME RESULTS. SEE HUMBUCKER COMPARISON DIAGRAM

FIGURE 9.31 Humbucker®/Single/Single. (Diagram provided by Seymour Duncan®)

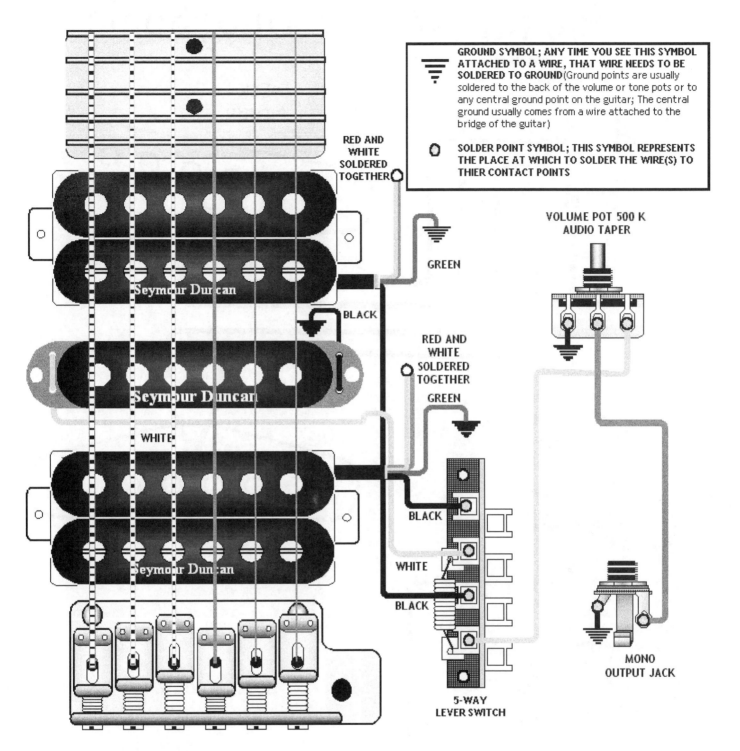

RED AND WHITE SOLDERED TOGETHER

GREEN

BLACK

RED AND WHITE SOLDERED TOGETHER

GREEN

WHITE

BLACK

WHITE

BLACK

VOLUME POT 500 K AUDIO TAPER

MONO OUTPUT JACK

5-WAY LEVER SWITCH

1 HUMBUCKER, 1 SINGLE COIL,1 HUMBUCKER,1 VOLUME 1 SELECTOR SWITCH

COPYRIGHT 2001 SEYMOUR DUNCAN / BASSLINES

THIS DIAGRAM SHOWS A 4-CONDUCTOR HUMBUCKER. YOU CAN USE A SINGLE CONDUCTOR HUMBUCKER SUCH AS A SH-55 SETH LOVER, SH-1 59' MODEL OR ANTIQUITY WITH THE SAME RESULTS. SEE HUMBUCKER COMPARISON DIAGRAM

FIGURE 9.32 Humbucker®/Single/Humbucker®. (Diagram provided by Seymour Duncan®)

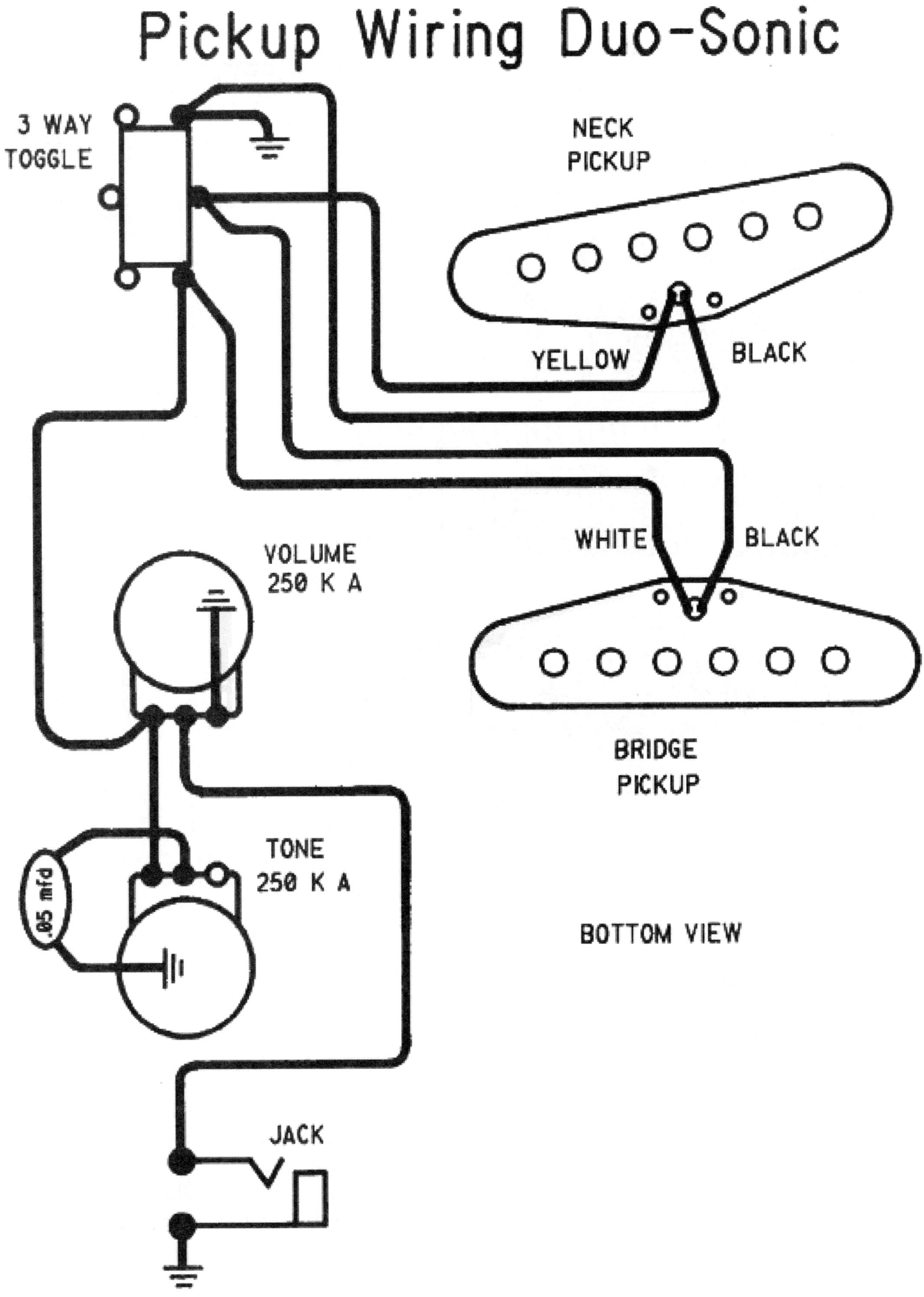

Pickup Wiring Duo-Sonic

FIGURE 9.33 Duo Sonic®. (Diagram provided by Seymour Duncan®)

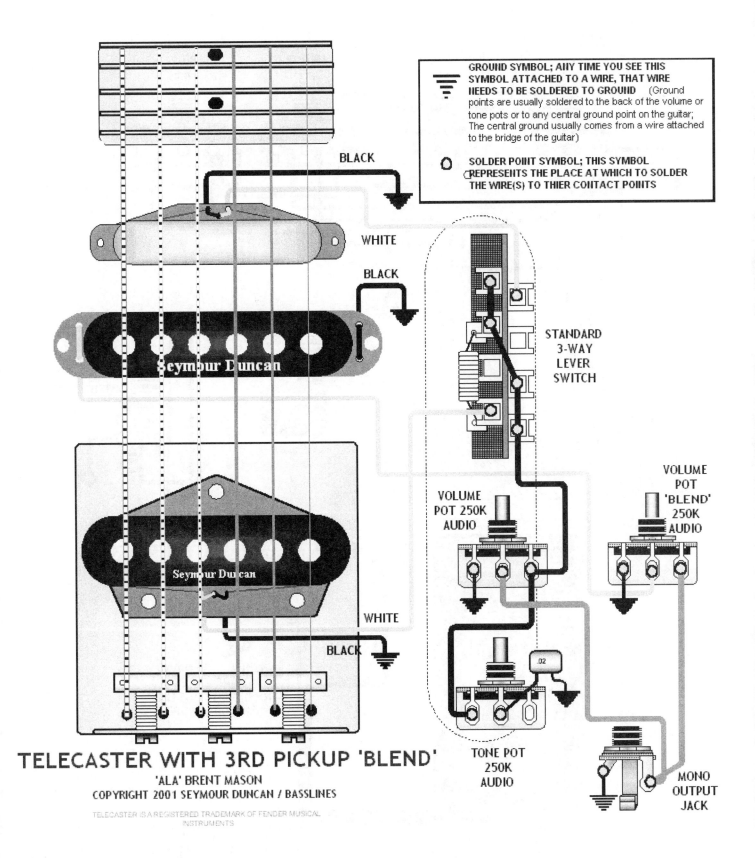

FIGURE 9.34 Tele® with three pickups and volume blend. (Diagram provided by Seymour Duncan®)

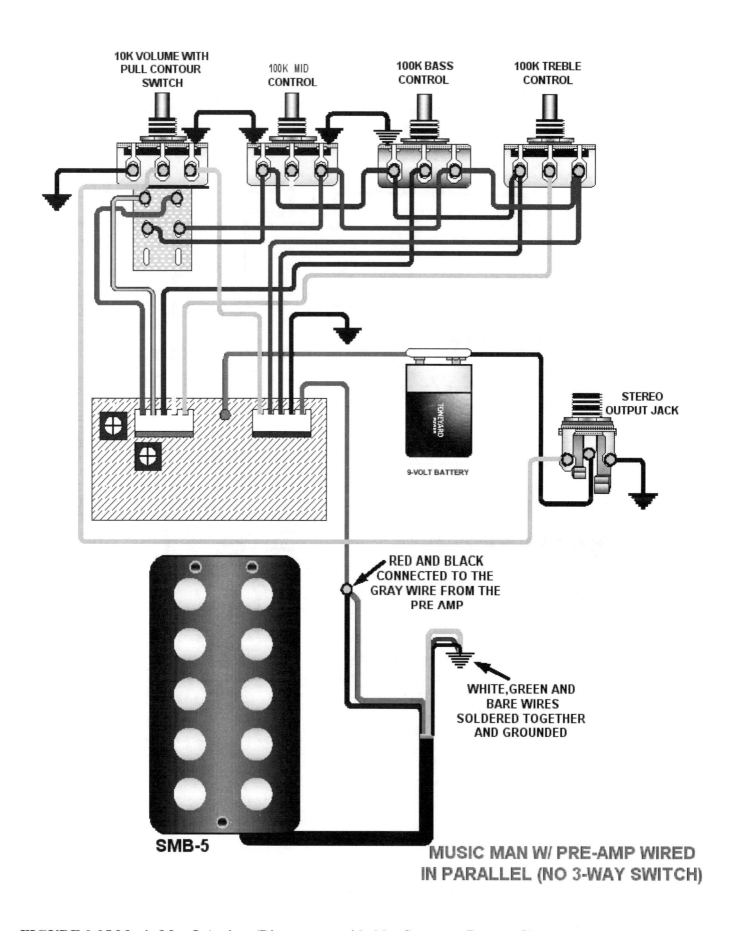

FIGURE 9.35 Music Man® Active. (Diagram provided by Seymour Duncan®)

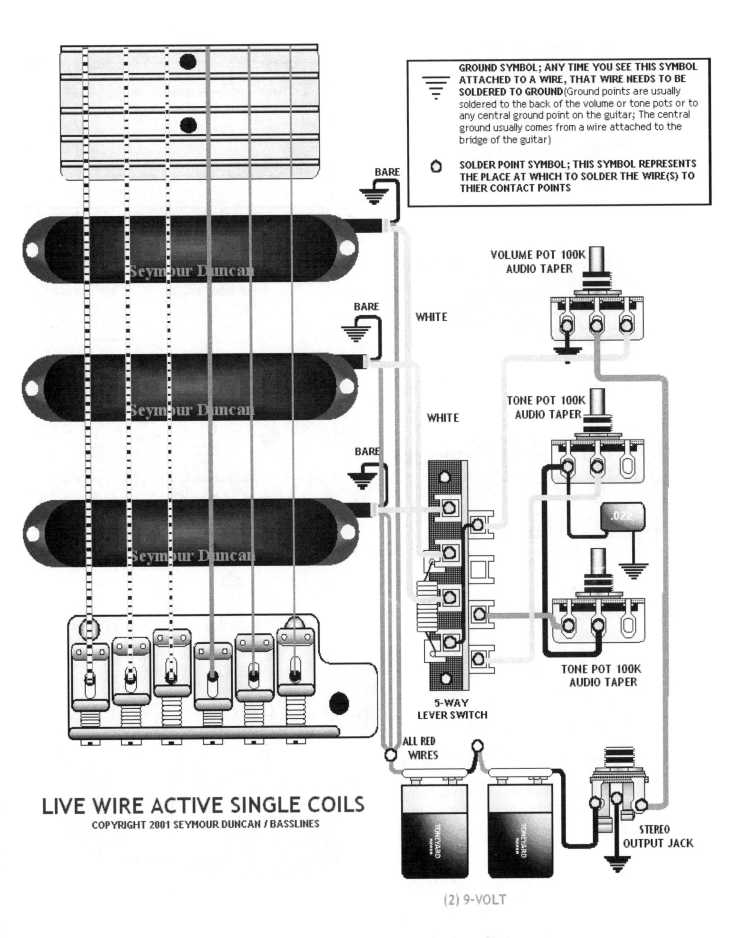

GROUND SYMBOL; ANY TIME YOU SEE THIS SYMBOL ATTACHED TO A WIRE, THAT WIRE NEEDS TO BE SOLDERED TO GROUND (Ground points are usually soldered to the back of the volume or tone pots or to any central ground point on the guitar; The central ground usually comes from a wire attached to the bridge of the guitar)

SOLDER POINT SYMBOL; THIS SYMBOL REPRESENTS THE PLACE AT WHICH TO SOLDER THE WIRE(S) TO THIER CONTACT POINTS

BARE

WHITE

VOLUME POT 100K
AUDIO TAPER

BARE

WHITE

TONE POT 100K
AUDIO TAPER

.022

BARE

5-WAY
LEVER SWITCH

TONE POT 100K
AUDIO TAPER

ALL RED
WIRES

STEREO
OUTPUT JACK

LIVE WIRE ACTIVE SINGLE COILS
COPYRIGHT 2001 SEYMOUR DUNCAN / BASSLINES

(2) 9-VOLT

FIGURE 9.36 Active Strat®. (Diagram provided by Seymour Duncan®)

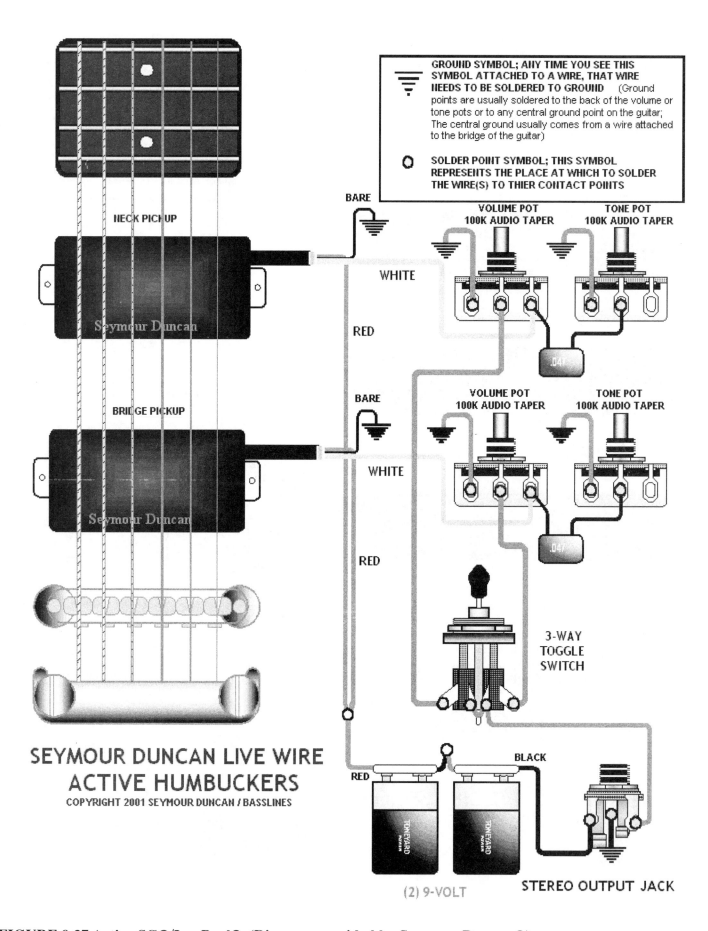

GROUND SYMBOL; ANY TIME YOU SEE THIS SYMBOL ATTACHED TO A WIRE, THAT WIRE NEEDS TO BE SOLDERED TO GROUND   (Ground points are usually soldered to the back of the volume or tone pots or to any central ground point on the guitar; The central ground usually comes from a wire attached to the bridge of the guitar)

SOLDER POINT SYMBOL; THIS SYMBOL REPRESENTS THE PLACE AT WHICH TO SOLDER THE WIRE(S) TO THIER CONTACT POINTS

NECK PICKUP

BRIDGE PICKUP

Seymour Duncan

Seymour Duncan

BARE

WHITE

RED

BARE

WHITE

RED

VOLUME POT
100K AUDIO TAPER

TONE POT
100K AUDIO TAPER

.047

VOLUME POT
100K AUDIO TAPER

TONE POT
100K AUDIO TAPER

.047

3-WAY
TOGGLE
SWITCH

SEYMOUR DUNCAN LIVE WIRE
ACTIVE HUMBUCKERS
COPYRIGHT 2001 SEYMOUR DUNCAN / BASSLINES

RED

BLACK

TONEYARD POWER

TONEYARD POWER

(2) 9-VOLT

STEREO OUTPUT JACK

FIGURE 9.37 Active SG®/Les Paul®. (Diagram provided by Seymour Duncan®)

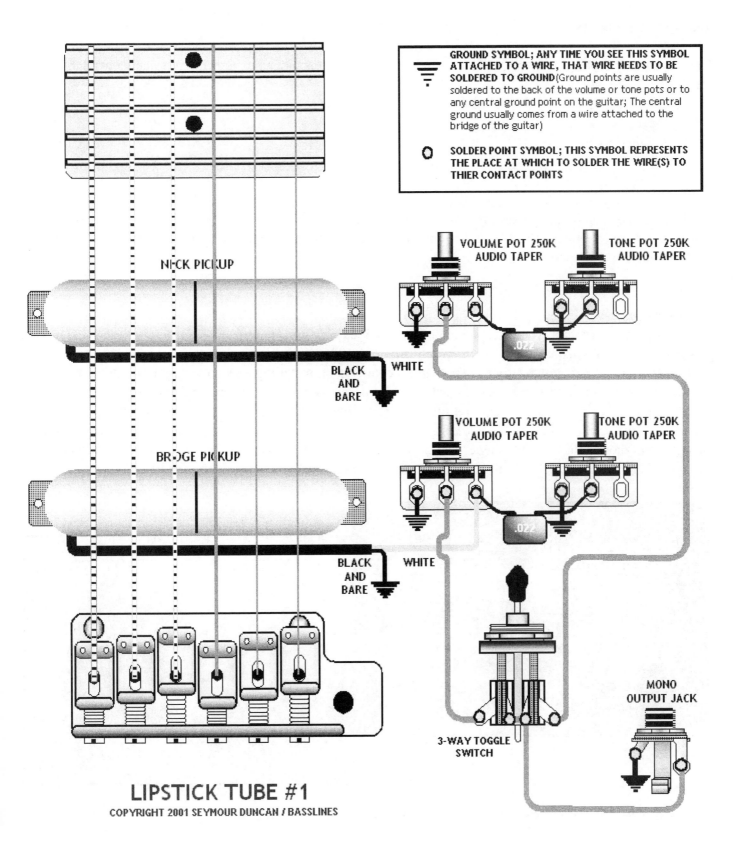

FIGURE 9.38 Lipstick Tube Pickup System. (Diagram provided by Seymour Duncan®)

Acoustic Pickups Systems

There are many types of systems available for an acoustic guitar. Four of the primary systems available today are:

1. Piezo
2. Magnetic
3. Microphone
4. Transducers

Each type can be combined into different systems to produce a broad dynamic range. All of these electronic mediums have a distinct application and sound. Some sound better active, some are better passive. Here is a breakdown on their function and application.

Piezo Pickups

The term piezo refers to a type of crystal. When it is under pressure, it emits an electronic signal. Piezo crystal pickups sound best when combined with an active preamp. The piezo pickup is commonly used in acoustic guitars and even in electric guitars as well. The biggest challenge in installing a piezo pickup is attaining even string balance. If the bridge saddle and the saddle slot are not perfectly flat or level (in relationship to each other), you won't have even string balance when you plug the guitar into an amp. The way you remedy this problem is to either re-cut the bridge saddle or the saddle slot, or both. If the bridge saddle fits rather loose, you may want to cut the bottom of the saddle at a slight angle. The angle should compensate for how far the saddle leans forward when the guitar is tuned to pitch. This will keep the contact and pressure even between the saddle and pickup.

FIGURE 9.39 A,B Piezo pickup system. (Photos provided by L.R. Baggs®)

Magnetic Pickups

Magnetic pickups are very similar to what you would find in an electric guitar, but modified to fit into the soundhole of an acoustic. String balance is also a challenge with magnetic pickups because the magnets pick up the treble strings much louder than the wound strings. The reason for this is because the wound strings are wrapped with bronze, which doesn't have a lot of magnetism. The plain or treble strings are steel; therefore, they are strongly attracted to the magnets.

FIGURE 9.40 Magnetic pickup system. (Photo provided by Seymour Duncan®)

Microphones are used mostly in the studio. However, many live performers use them inside their instruments to add a different dynamic to their sound. The microphone will produce the most life-like reproduction of your guitar's acoustic sound. The biggest challenge to having a mic in your guitar is feedback. Unless you can turn the mic off in your monitor, there is a high likelihood that it will feedback. The reason for the feedback is because the body of the guitar acts like a parabolic reflector and amplifies the signal. Add to that the monitor facing the guitar (and the mic) and the result sounds like a stuck pig in a rail yard. There are systems that combine a microphone with a piezo pickup and can be run "stereo". In other words, using a stereo "Y" cable, the tip (piezo pickup) will go to one channel on the mixer, and the ring microphone will go to another channel on the mixer. Then the microphone can be turned off in the monitor, but left on in the house mix. The piezo will be left on in both the monitor and the house mix. This way, the audience hears an amazing reproduction of the guitar and the player hears a solid signal without any feedback.

FIGURE 9.41 Microphones. (Photo provided by L.R. Baggs®)

Transducer pickups are activated by vibrations and movement. Some of the transducers attach to the top of the guitar inside the body. Other systems are placed under the bridge saddle. Transducers are very dynamic, but can also be prone to feedback.

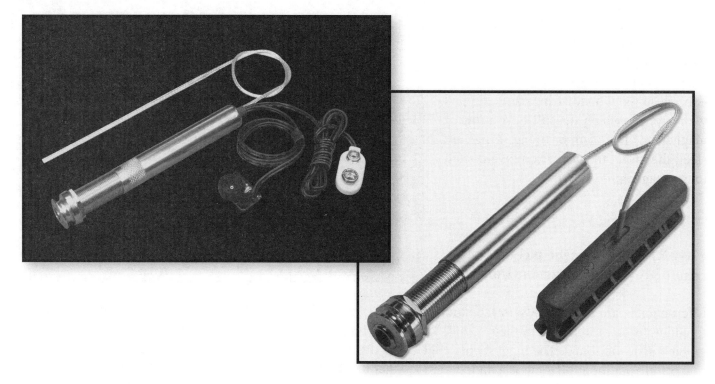

FIGURE 9.42A,B Transducer pickup system. (Photos provided by L.R. Baggs®)

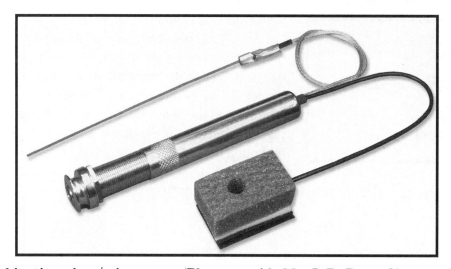

FIGURE 9.43 Combination piezo/mic system. (Photo provided by L.R. Baggs®)

Some systems combine some or all of these systems. It's all part of the never-ending quest for ultimate tone and balance.

Troubleshooting and Solutions

Pickup failure can be caused by several different reasons. Here are a few of them.

Electric Pickup Failure:
- Broken winding in coil
- Broken lead wire
- Corroded windings
- De-gaussed magnets
- Wired wrong

Acoustic Pickup Failure:
- Broken piezo crystal
- Rip in shielding surrounding the piezo crystal
- Separation between contacts in transducer
- Broken wires
- Bad preamp

When a magnetic pickup fails, usually the coil needs to be rewound or needs new magnets. Only a professional should attempt this, unless, you have the proper equipment. Once in a while you will get lucky and find that one of the pickup leads are broken. In this case, simply solder it back on.

As for an acoustic guitar pickup, you are better off replacing the components.

Top 10 Signs of a Problematic Guitar

Before you purchase an instrument, make sure that you completely inspect it before you buy it. It is always a good idea to bring along someone who can identify serious problems and defects when you shop for an instrument. Many repair shops offer an "evaluation" or "inspection" for a small fee. It's better to pay $20 or $30 to find a serious problem before you buy, than to spend over a thousand on an instrument that needs an overhaul.

Electric Guitar

1. Won't play in tune.
2. Worn string nut.
3. Fret wear.
4. Bad neck angle.
5. Electronics malfunction.
6. Cracked or stripped bridge saddles.
7. Loose or uneven frets.
8. Uneven fretboard.
9. Broken trussrod.
10. Broken headstock.

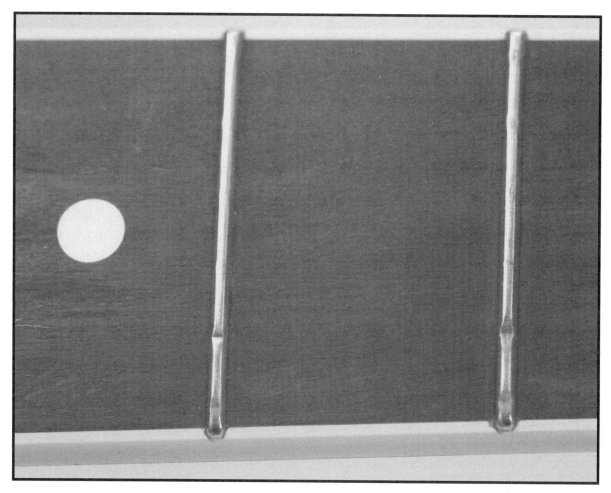

FIGURE 10.1 Frets become flat and develop an almost diamond shape dent as they wear. (Photo by Skip Anderson)

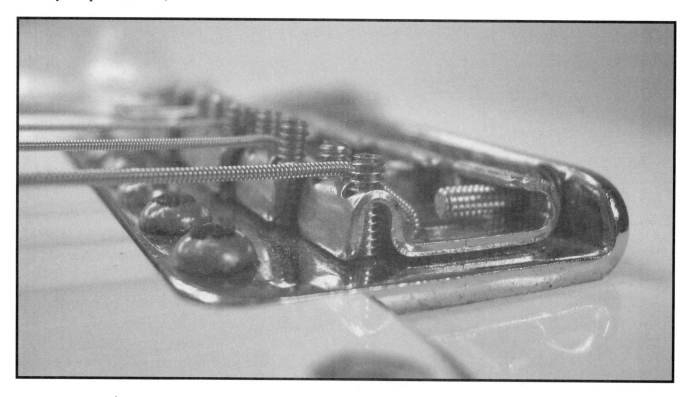

FIGURE 10.2 A low neck angle is easily identified because the guitar will have high action even if the bridge and saddles are as low as they can go. (Photo by John LeVan)

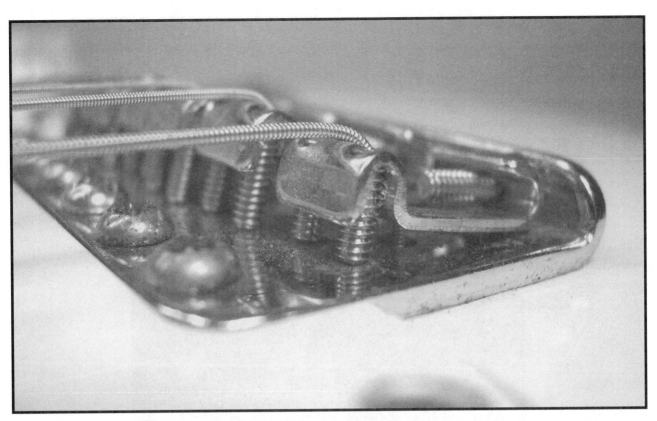

FIGURE 10.3 A high neck angle is easily identified because the guitar will have very low action even if the bridge and saddles are as high as they can go. (Photo by John LeVan)

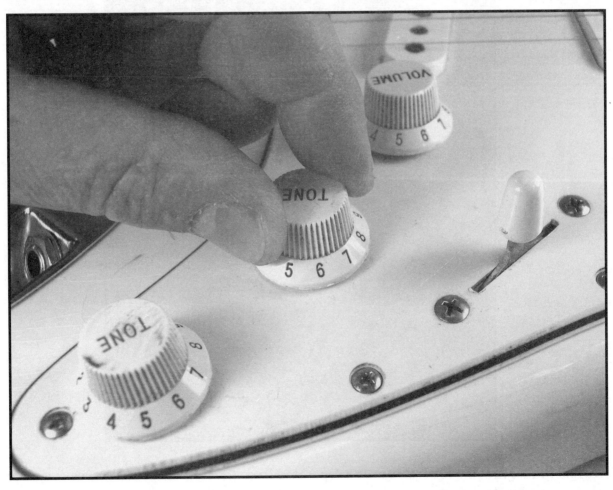

FIGURE 10.4 Always test the electronics in a guitar before you buy it. (Photo by John LeVan)

FIGURE 10.5 Inspect the hardware and make sure it isn't rusted, chipped or cracked. (Photo by John LeVan)

FIGURE 10.6 Make sure that the frets haven't separated from the fretboard, this can be very expensive to repair. (Photo by Skip Anderson)

If the fretboard is wavy or looks uneven, it probably needs a plane and refret.

Broken trussrods are detected by attempting to adjust them and then checking the results.

FIGURE 10.7 Look carefully for any sign of a crack or a repaired crack. Even though a properly repaired headstock will last decades, the fact that it was broken devalues the guitar by as much as 50 percent. (Photo by Skip Anderson)

Acoustic Guitar

1. Won't play in tune.
2. Fret wear.
3. Worn string nut.
4. Cracked bridge.
5. Sharp fret ends.
6. Loose braces.
7. Worn bridge plate.
8. Worn-out bridge pin holes.
9. Body cracks.
10. Bad neck angle.

In order for a guitar to intonate properly, the saddles, nut and frets must be in the correct location.

FIGURE 10.8 Fretwork is time consuming and expensive. (Photo by Skip Anderson)

The string nut usually erodes from the face (fret side) to the back. This can also cause the guitar to play out of tune.

FIGURE 10.9 Closely inspect the bridge for cracks which can also be a telltale sign of a broken bridgeplate or brace. (Photo by John LeVan)

FIGURE 10.10 If the fretends are sharp, the guitar may be dried out and needs to be humidified. (Photo by Skip Anderson)

You can usually tell if a top brace is loose by looking for a ripple or crease in the top.

To check the back braces, gently press on the back along the brace and listen for a creaking noise or a popping sound.

FIGURE 10.11 The easiest way to identify a worn out pin plate is to look at the bridge where the pins go in. If the wrap of the string is against or on top of the saddle, the bridge plate is probably worn out. (Photo by John LeVan)

If the bridge pins fall out of the bridge while the guitar has strings on it, the pins are loose. This problem can be fixed by either replacing the bridge and/or bridge plate or buying oversized bridge pins.

FIGURE 10.12 Body cracks can be deceiving; use abundant natural light when you inspect the body. (Photo by Skip Anderson)

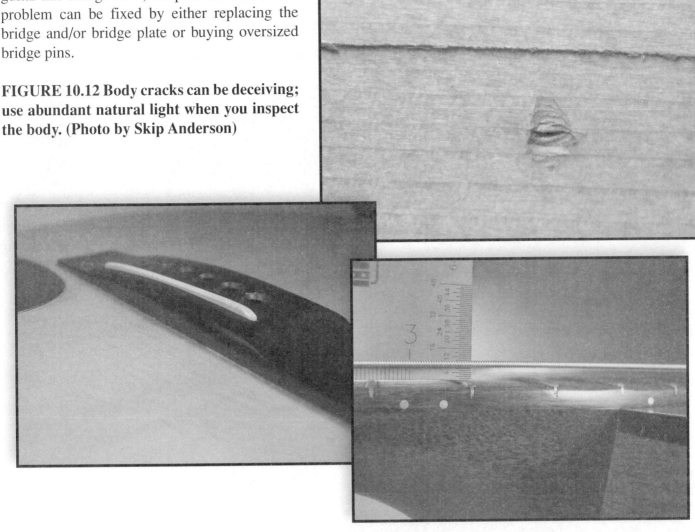

FIGURE 10.13A,B A low neck angle is easily identified because the guitar will have high action even if the bridge and saddle are as low as they can go. (Photos by John LeVan)

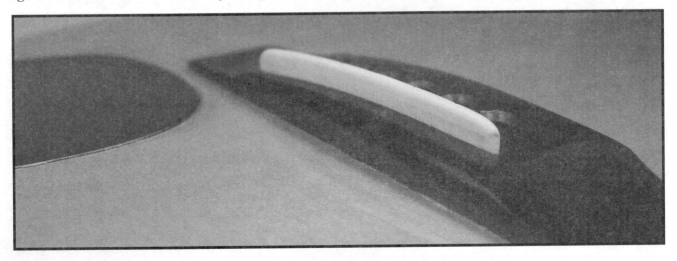

FIGURE 10.14 A high neck angle is easily identified because the guitar will have low action and a very tall saddle. (Photo by John LeVan)

With the information discussed in the previous chapters of this book, you should be able to identify each of these problems by thoroughly inspecting the instrument you are considering. Many of these ailments are very expensive to repair, so be very attentive and meticulous when you conduct your inspection.

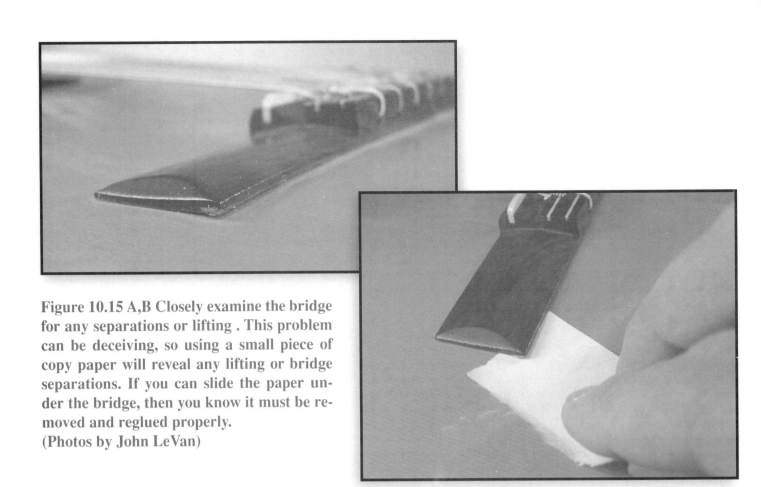

Figure 10.15 A,B Closely examine the bridge for any separations or lifting . This problem can be deceiving, so using a small piece of copy paper will reveal any lifting or bridge separations. If you can slide the paper under the bridge, then you know it must be removed and reglued properly.
(Photos by John LeVan)

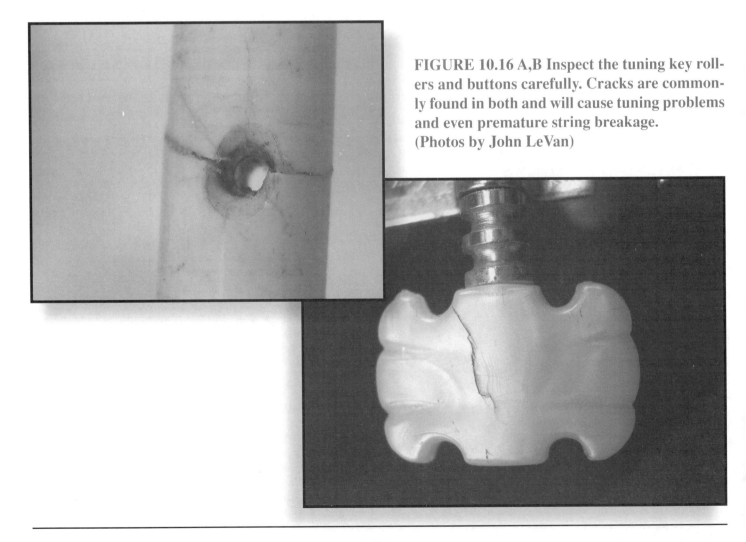

FIGURE 10.16 A,B Inspect the tuning key rollers and buttons carefully. Cracks are commonly found in both and will cause tuning problems and even premature string breakage.
(Photos by John LeVan)

Other Upgrades and Repairs

There are several ways to upgrade and improve your guitar's performance without detracting from its value. Below are a few examples of how to upgrade your instrument.

Installing a Strap Button

List of Components

- Neck
- Heel
- Strap Button
- Button Screw
- Felt Washer
- 3/32" Drill Bit
- Drill
- Medium-Tip Phillips Screwdriver
- Large-Tip Phillips Screwdriver

The installation of a strap button is a relatively easy project, as long as you follow a few basic steps.

1. Determine the best location to install the strap button.
2. Mark the location with the screw.
3. Pre-drill the screw hole for the strap button.
4. Gently countersink the finish around the screw hole using the medium and then large-tip Phillips screw driver.
5. Push screw through the strap button and add the felt washer at the end.
6. Screw the strap button screw into the heel with a screwdriver.

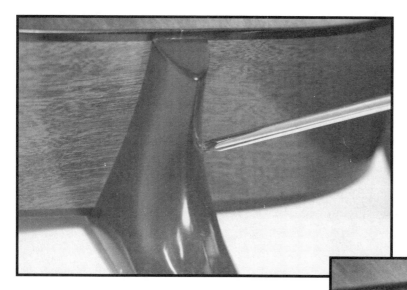

FIGURE 11.1 Location is everything. I recommend installing the button 1 1/2" below the fretboard on the treble side of the neck. If the button is installed too low on the heel, the guitar will tilt away from you when you use your guitar strap. If you place the button too high, your hand will bump it when you play on the higher frets. Once you have determined the proper location to install the strap button, gently mark it with your medium-tip Phillips screwdriver. Be careful not to slip and scratch the neck. (Photo by Skip Anderson)

FIGURE 11.2 Using a 3/32" drill bit, drill a hole into the neck to the depth of the screw only. It is also important to drill the hole at the same angle as the screw, perpendicular to the heel. (Photo by Skip Anderson)

FIGURE 11.3 Using your medium-tip Phillips screwdriver, spin the handle while gently countersinking the finish around the hole. Then use a large-tip Phillips screwdriver. Don't bore into the wood too far; you only need to countersink the finish enough for the screw to clear it. This will prevent any finish from peeling up when you install the screw. (Photo by Skip Anderson)

FIGURE 11.4 Insert the screw into the strap button and add the felt washer to the end of the screw. Screw the strap button screw into the heel and you are finished. Make sure that you don't over-tighten the screw. It can strip the wood if you torque the screw too much.
(Photo by Skip Anderson)

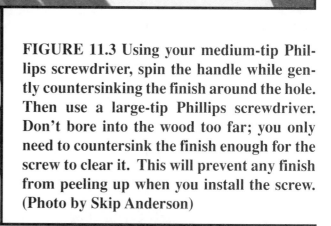

Tuning Keys

List of Components

- Headstock
- Tuning Keys
- Mounting Screws
- Tuning Key Hole
- Tuning Key Button
- Tuning Key Post
- Screw-in Collar
- Press-in Collar

The quality of your tuning keys will make a big difference in respect to your guitar's ability to stay in tune. The higher the turning ratio, the better it will tune. In other words, the more times you have to turn the button to achieve one revolution of the tuning key post, the finer the tuning. The turning ratio of most tuning keys will range from 11:1 to 18:1. 11:1 to 14:1 is a terrible turning ratio. 15:1 up to 16:1 is a good turning ratio. 18:1 and up, is an excellent turning ratio.

Matching the correct key to your guitar is important. There are many different types of keys on the market. Whether your guitar has a set of vintage keys or the latest locking keys, chances are you will find a set that will be an exact retrofit for your guitar. I recommend that you only use keys that are an exact retrofit so that you don't have to alter the guitar to install them. Altering a guitar to replace the keys will adversely affect the value of a guitar. Brands like Gotoh® and Schaller® offer a wide range of tuning keys with good to excellent turning ratios and affordable prices. They range in price from $35 up to $125.

Tuning Key Installation

There are a few basic tools needed to replace tuning keys.

Tool List

- Cordless Drill with Small-Tip Phillips
- 10mm Deep-Well Socket (optional)
- Knob Puller (optional)

FIGURE 11.5 Small Phillips tip along with your cordless drill is perfect to remove the tuning key screws that hold the keys to the headstock. (Photo by John LeVan)

FIGURE 11.6 A 10mm deep-well socket is the perfect size for most tuning keys with a screw-in collar. If the tuning keys have press-in collars (bushings), you won't need this tool. (Photo by John LeVan)

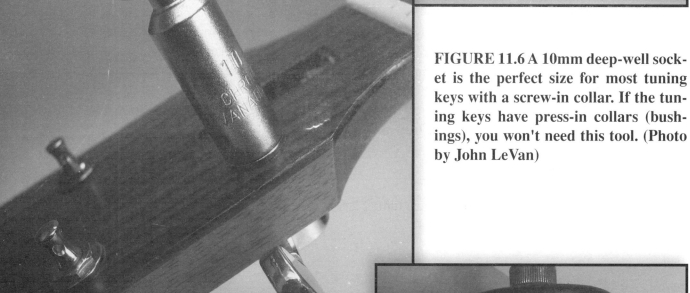

FIGURE 11.7 A knob puller is only necessary if you need to remove press-in bushings. If the bushings will work with the new keys, don't remove them. If the old bushings are too small, you will need to remove them from the instrument and install the new set provided by the tuning key manufacturer. (Photo by John LeVan)

Keep in mind the risk in removing a press-in bushing. It is very easy to chip or lift the finish around the bushing. Unless absolutely necessary, avoid removing press-in bushings.

Here are the simple steps for removing the tuning keys.

1. Remove the strings from the guitar.
2. Remove the screws holding the tuning keys to the headstock.
3. Remove (if applicable) the threaded collar that surrounds the tuning key post.
4. Slide the tuning keys out of the headstock.

When removing the screws from the tuning keys (on the backside of the headstock), be careful not to strip them. You may want to set your cordless drill on a slower setting.

FIGURE 11.8 If the tuning keys have a screw-in collar, remove it. Not all tuning keys require the same tools when replacing them, so make sure you use the right tool for the job. (Photo by John LeVan)

FIGURE 11.9 The tuning keys should slide right out of the peg holes in the headstock. (Photo by John LeVan)

When installing the new tuning keys, be sure that they match up with the original equipment you have just removed. If the new keys don't fit into the original peg-holes, don't force them. You may not have the right keys.

FIGURE 11.10 If the old keys have press-in bushings that are smaller than the new bushings, you will need to remove the old bushings and install new ones. This is only recommended if absolutely necessary. You risk damaging the finish on the face of the headstock every time you remove one of the bushings.
(Photo by John LeVan)

FIGURE 11.11 When installing a tuning key with a threaded collar, do not overtighten the collar. The collar can easily strip, ruining the tuning key. The collar only needs to be "finger" tight. There is no reason to torque it down with excessive pressure. (Photo by John LeVan)

After installing the new tuning keys, restring the guitar and you're in business. The most important points I can stress to you are:

- Use keys that are an exact retrofit.
- Always use the correct tool for the job.
- Never over-torque a screw or treaded collar.

Classical Key Installation

FIGURE ll.12 Small Phillips tip along with your cordless drill is perfect to remove the tuning key screws that hold the keys to the headstock. (Photo by John LeVan)

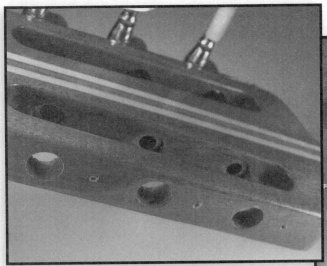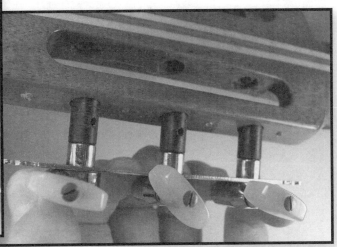

FIGURE 11.13 A,B The tuning keys should slide right out of the peg-holes in the headstock. (Photos by John Levan)

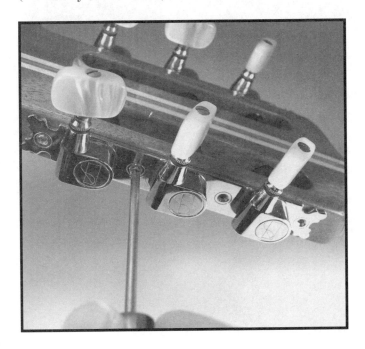

FIGURE 11.14 When installing new tuning keys, do not overtighten the screws. This can easily strip out the hole and/or the screw head. There is no reason to torque it down with excessive pressure. (Photo by John LeVan)

Bridge Pins

Two common problems with bridge pins are:

1.   Too loose
2.   Too tight

If the bridge pins are too loose, you should either replace them with oversized bridge pins, or take your guitar to a qualified luthier. When bridge pins are too loose it's generally because the bridge pins, bridge pin holes in the bridge, and/or bridge plate, have worn out. The result is loose bridge pins.

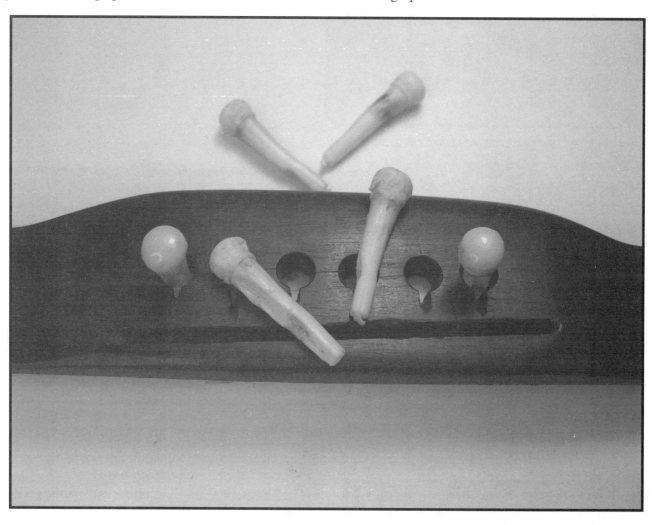

FIGURE 11.15 Here is an example of a bridge with worn-out bridge pin holes and pins. (Photo by John LeVan)

If the bridge pins are too tight, it's because the bridge pin holes are too small. A small tapered ream is the right tool to correct this problem. If the bridge pin holes aren't reamed to the correct size, it can result in broken bridge pins and even a cracked bridge.

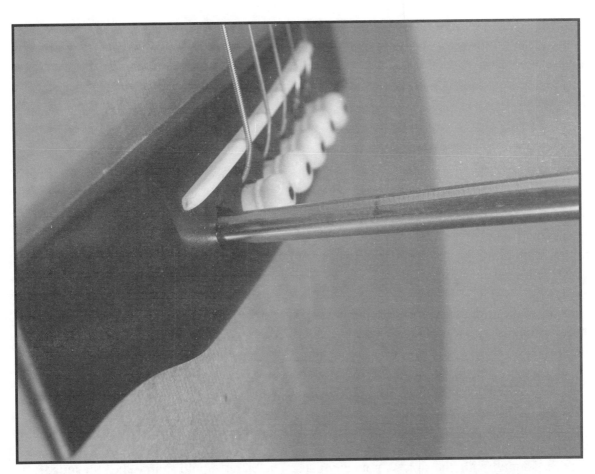

FIGURE 11.16 Gently ream out the bridge pin holes, checking them frequently for a proper fit. If you have to force the bridge pin into the hole, it is probably too tight. (Photo by Skip Anderson)

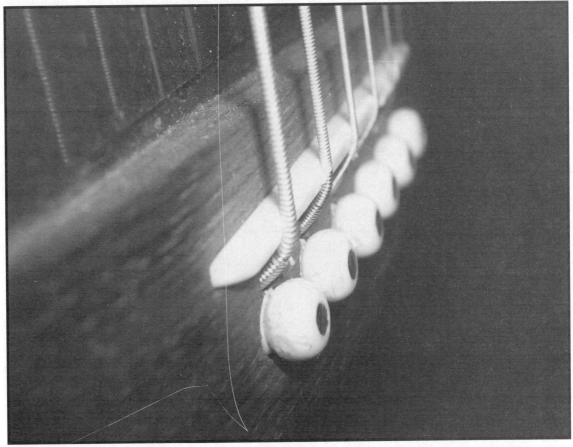

FIGURE 11.17 Here is an example of properly fitted bridge pins. (Photo by John LeVan)

Bone String Nut

A bone string nut will improve sustain and tone of almost any guitar. Carving one isn't easy. It requires a lot of practice and patience. Here is what you need to get started.

Tool and Materials List

- 100-Grit Sandpaper
- 1500-Grit Sandpaper
- Nut File Set
- Mechanical Pencil
- Super Glue® Accelerator
- Magnifying Lamp
- Fretting Hammer
- Bone Blank

- 220-Grit Sandpaper
- Flat Surface
- Needle File Set
- Thin Super Glue®
- Q-Tips®
- Scale (rule)
- Flathead Screwdriver

Before you start, make sure that you have a good piece of bone to start with. If it is porous, cracked or too oily, you may have problems with it functioning properly as a string nut. Here are step-by-step instructions on carving a new string nut.

1. Remove the old nut (see Chapter 5) with a flathead screwdriver and a fretting hammer.
2. Clean out the nut slot (see Chapter 5) using your needle files.
3. Sand the nut blank to the proper width. Use the 100-grit paper to remove a lot of material and the 220-grit paper to remove just a little. The 1500-grit paper is for polishing the nut blank. Make sure that the blank fits squarely into the slot, without any gaps. The blank should fit into the slot snug.
4. Mark the edges of the nut blank with your mechanical pencil to show how much material you need remove to make it flush with the sides of the fretboard.
5. Sand one side of the nut blank, first with 220-grit, then with 1500-grit sandpaper until it is flush with the fretboard.
6. Repeat Step 5 on the other side of the nut blank.
7. Lay your scale (rule) flat on top of the frets with the edge against the face of the nut blank. Mark the blank with your pencil along the scale from the treble side to the bass side of the blank. This is your guide to keep you from carving into the nut too far.
8. Remove the nut blank and sand the top of it down to the pencil line (you may want to leave a little extra material on the bass side). Shape the top of the blank so that it slopes (angles) towards the headstock.
9. Using your magnifying lamp, pencil and your scale (rule), measure out the string spacing on the nut blank. Generally, the two E strings are 1/8" from the edge of the fretboard. Be sure to measure from the outside of the string, not the center of the string. The rest of the strings are generally 1/4" apart (give or take 1/64"). Classical as well as some steel-stringed guitars have wider string spacing. Make sure to measure the spacing of the strings on the old nut to get an idea of what the spacing should be for the new one. Next, mark the location of each string slot on the nut blank with your pencil, in accordance with the actual width of the strings. The object of the exercise is to place each string the same distance from the other (based on the outside dimensions of the string, not the center).
10. Cut the string slots (shallow); now is a good time to install the strings and tune them to pitch.
11. Measure the distance from the edge of the fretboard to the E strings as well as the distance between the strings. Adjust them accordingly and finish cutting the string slots to the proper depth.
12. Remove the strings, secure the nut with a drop of Super Glue® (to the face of the nut), and polish with 1500-grit sandpaper and a polishing cloth.
13. Restring.

FIGURE 11.18 Make sure the nut blank fits in the slot, square and flush. (Photo by John LeVan)

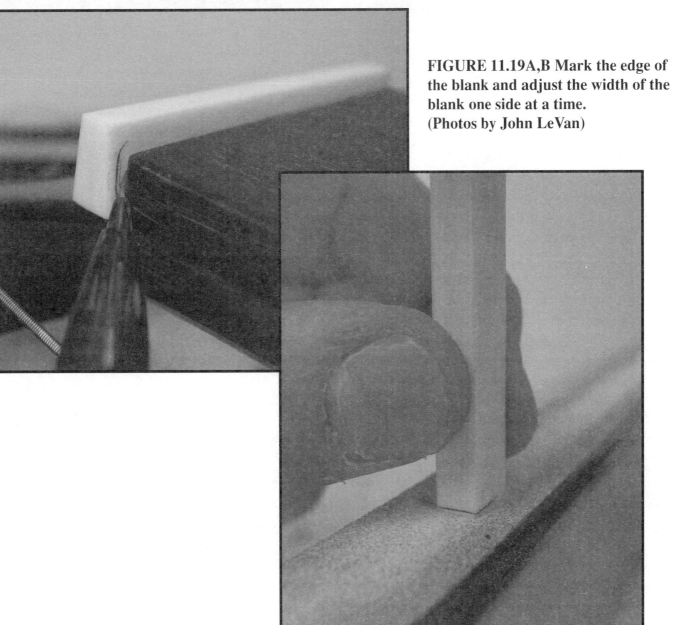

FIGURE 11.19A,B Mark the edge of the blank and adjust the width of the blank one side at a time. (Photos by John LeVan)

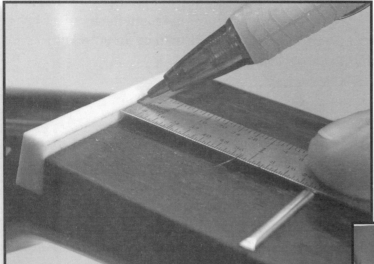

FIGURE 11.20 To measure the height of the nut, lay your scale on top of the frets and mark the face of the nut with a pencil.
(Photo by John LeVan)

FIGURE 11.21 A Sand the excess material off of the top of the nut blank and reshape.
(Photo by John LeVan)

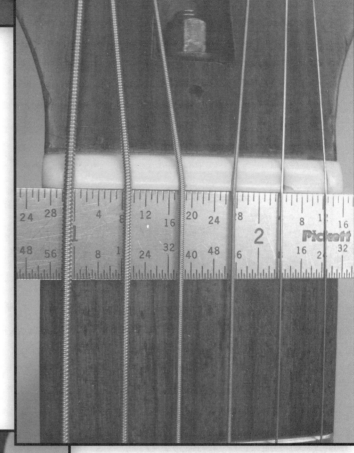

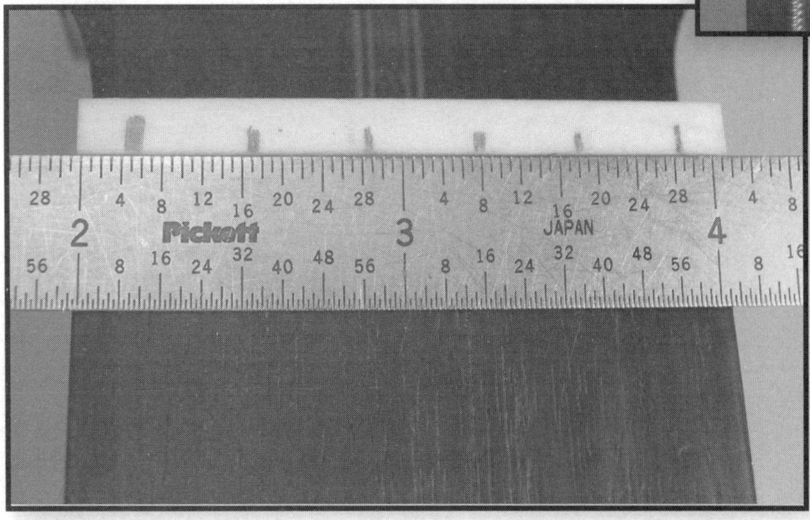

FIGURE 11.22 Measure to proper distance for each string in relationship to the fretboard and adjoining strings.
(Photo by John LeVan)

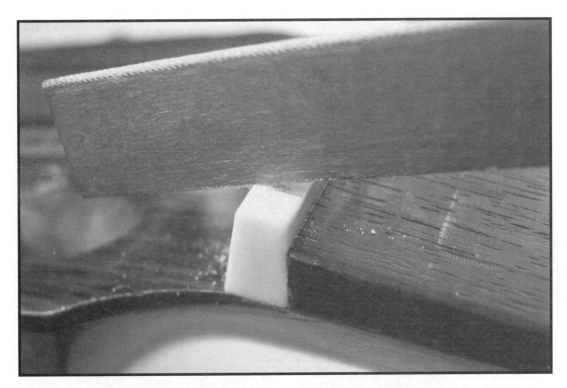

FIGURE 11.23 Carve shallow slots into the nut blank and restring. (Photo by John LeVan)

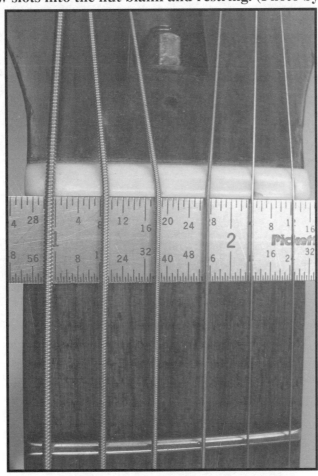

FIGURE 11.24 Shore-up the distances of the slots and cut them to the proper depth and distance. (Photo by John LeVan)

The spacing on a Dobro® is about the same as an acoustic, but the action is much higher. Polish the string nut.

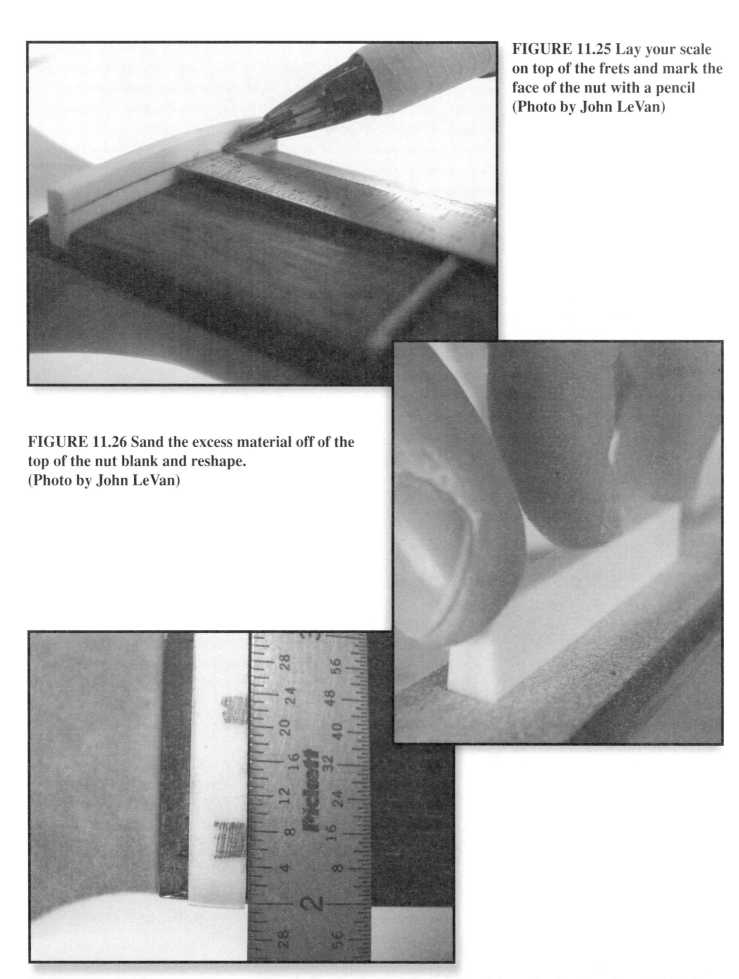

FIGURE 11.25 Lay your scale on top of the frets and mark the face of the nut with a pencil (Photo by John LeVan)

FIGURE 11.26 Sand the excess material off of the top of the nut blank and reshape. (Photo by John LeVan)

FIGURE 11.27 Measure to proper distance for each string in relationship to the fretboard and adjoining strings. On a bass guitar the distance from string to string is much greater than an electric or acoustic. (Photo by John LeVan)

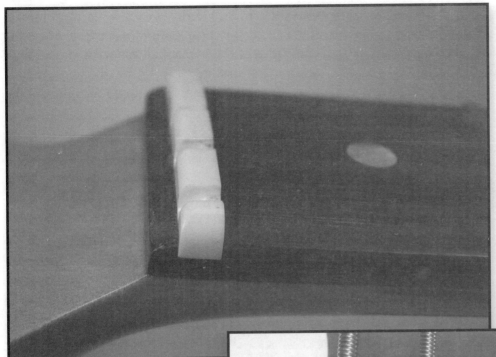

FIGURE 11.28 Carve shallow slots into the nut blank and restring.
(Photo by John LeVan)

FIGURE 11.29 Shore-up the distances of the slots and cut them to the proper depth and distance.
(Photo by John LeVan)

FIGURE 11.30 Sand the excess material off the top of the nut blank and reshape. Notice the curvature of the bottom of this string nut. Many electric guitars have a 7 1/4" radius on the bottom of their string nut to match the radius of the nut slot.
(Photo by John LeVan)

FIGURE 11.31 Measure to proper distance for each string in relationship to the fretboard and adjoining strings. Distance between the strings on an electric guitar is much tighter compared to an acoustic or classical guitar.
(Photo by John LeVan)

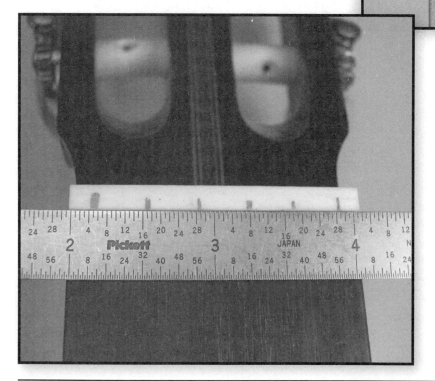

FIGURE 11.32 Measure to proper distance for each string in relationship to the fretboard and adjoining strings. A classical guitar will have a wider string spacing than steel stringed guitars.
(Photo by John LeVan)

FIGURE 11.33 Shore-up the distances of the slots and cut them to the proper depth and distance. (Photo by John LeVan)

Compensated Bone Saddle

A compensated bone saddle will also improve the volume, sustain and tone of most fine acoustic guitars. "Compensated" simply means that it is properly intonated or adjusted in order to play more in tune. As with a string nut, choose a good bone blank before you start. Here are step-by-step instructions on carving a compensated bone saddle.

Tool and Materials List

- 100-Grit Sandpaper
- 220-Grit Sandpaper
- 1500-Grit Sandpaper
- Flat Surface
- Needle File Set
- Mechanical Pencil
- Scale (rule)
- Bone Blank

Here are the step-by-step instructions.

1. Remove the old saddle. If the old saddle fits the saddle slot well, use it for a template.
2. Place the old saddle against the new saddle blank on a flat surface. Trace the outline of the old saddle on the new saddle with your pencil.
3. Sand the new blank to match the old saddle's width, height and radius.
4. Place the new saddle blank into the saddle slot and begin carving the top of the saddle to match the angle of each string. Make sure that you pay close attention to the intonation.
5. Polish the saddle with 1500-grit sandpaper and a polishing cloth.
6. Restring.

FIGURE 11.34 Use your old saddle to trace the new saddle. (Photo by John LeVan)

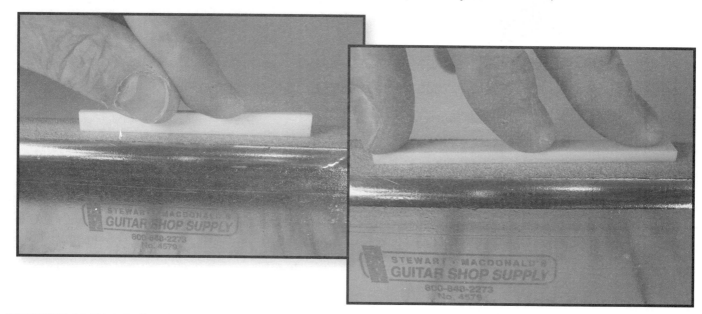

FIGURE 11.35 A,B Sand the new blank to proper size. (Photos by John LeVan)

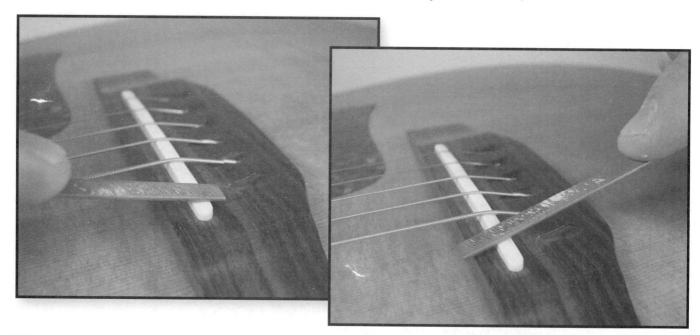

FIGURE 11.36 A,B Carve the angles for each string and intonate. (Photos by John LeVan)
Polish the saddle using 1500-grit sandpaper. Your new bone saddle should be smooth and clean.

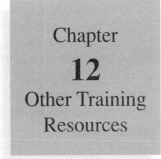

Other Training Resources

There are several sources of training available to aspiring luthiers. Apprenticeships, factory training and workshops are three of the best ways I know to learn and develop old and new skills. I have been fortunate enough to have experienced all three through other repair techs, luthiers, luthier guilds and manufacturers. I recommend these resources to anyone who wants to learn more about this ancient and fascinating trade.

Apprenticeships

The ancient tradition of apprenticeship is still alive and a great way to learn a skill or trade. An apprenticeship begins with the basics; sweeping floors, polishing guitars and taking out the trash. Eventually, you get to watch the master practice his or her craft and ask a few questions. It is best to keep a journal during your apprenticeship. There are always new questions and more profound answers. The more you learn, the more there is to know. Before you know it, you're in the middle of a neck reset or a bridge reglue on a vintage guitar. An apprenticeship will cost you a lot of time, but it is worth it. You get back what you invest, so invest wisely.

Factory Training

Factory training for me was like working in an emergency room. I was amazed at how fast and accurate these guys worked. I thought I was efficient until I spent some time with the repair techs at the Taylor Guitar® factory. It was a crash course in everything from top replacement to bridge reglues to neck resets. It was an amazing adventure. Factory training is one of the best ways to learn fundamental repair skills.

Workshops

When I was in Northern California, I was a part of a luthiers guild. We organized workshops and training seminars as well as swap meets. It was a great way to co-op with other luthiers to buy parts, tools and materials at a volume discount. There was always something to teach, learn and rediscover for me at the guild meetings. This is a great way to network with other luthiers to help carry on this great craft.

I sincerely hope that you found this book to be educational, enlightening and inspirational. I offer my best wishes to you in all of your lutherie pursuits.

If you want formal training on the procedures outlined in this book, you may contact me in one of the following ways;
email: guitarservices@aol.com
website: www.guitarservices.com
phone: 615-251-8884

John M. LeVan

Glossary

0000 Steel Wool, long, hairlike shavings of steel used for cleaning, polishing and smoothing. 0000 (ultra fine) refers to the grit or cut of the steel wool.

Action, movement of parts, or mechanisms. In reference to the guitar, the playability of, and/or the height of the strings in relationship to the neck.

Action Gauge®, tool engineered to measure the action of the guitar.

Active Electronics, electronic pickup system that requires a power source (batteries) to operate. Generally includes a pickup, preamp and battery.

Alligator Clip, a clip with strong, movable and toothed jaw designed to hold wires while they are being soldered.

Apprenticeship, period of training, study of a craft with a master craftsman.

Attack, velocity of strike; amount of force used to make a sound.

Binding, the wrap or gird around the body and/or neck of an instrument.

Biscuit, bridge support for a Dobro® or Resonator.

Bobbin, a reel or spool of thin, copper wire. Part of a magnetic pickup.

Bolt-on Neck, guitar neck that attaches with bolts instead of glue.

Braces, truss-like supports used to re-enforce the top and back of an acoustic instrument.

Bridge, mechanical or stationary base that holds the strings of a guitar.

Bridge Pin, pin that secures a string in place on a guitar.

Bridge Plate, wooden plate that holds the ball end of a string in place and supports the top of an acoustic instrument under the bridge.

Bridge Saddle, a thin arched support inserted into the bridge that separates the strings from the bridge on an acoustic instrument.

Burnishing, a form of polishing using a steel rod, or ultra-fine abrasives.

Coil, multiple wraps of thin copper wire on a pickup.

Coil Tap, splitting or tapping a coil. Decreasing the volume of a pickup by half.

Color Codes, system of symbols or colors used to explain the uses of specific leads (wires) in relationship to each other.

Conditioning, saturation and treatment of wood.

Cone, an aluminum, cone-shaped wedge used to amplify the sound of a resonator guitar or Dobro®.

Crown, top or peak of a fret.

Cutaway, an area of the upper bout on the treble side of a guitar that has been removed or cut away to give the player easier access to the higher notes on the neck.

Cyanoacrylite, transparent, thermoplastic resin containing cyanogens. Super Glue®.

Cyanoacrylite Accelerator, sprayable liquid that accelerates the drying of Super Glue®.

Cyanoacrylite Solvent, acetone based liquid that removes Super Glue®.

DPDT, Double-pole/Double-throw switch containing six terminals, two isolated common (output) terminals in the center of the switch, usually side by side. Each of the common terminals, located on either end of the switch in two rows, can be used to make contact with either one or two other terminals.

Draw, the degree of lift or play between the body of an electric guitar and the back of its tremolo.

Drift, settling or variance of a note shortly after it is struck.

Electronic Cleaner, chemical solution used to clean out dust and dirt from electronic components.

Feedback, high-pitched, microphonic frequencies produced by loose wires vibrating against each other.

Finish, end of a coil or winding.

Flat, level on top; lower than the desired pitch. Opposite of "sharp."

Flush, even or level.

Flush-cut Dykes (large), cutting pliers that cut fret ends flush or even.

Flush-cut Dykes (small), cutting pliers that cut flush or even. Used to remove frets from a fretboard.

Fret, metal composite containing zinc, silver and nickel shaped like a semicircle with a barbed stem.

Fret Bender, mechanical device used to bend fret wire to a specified degree or radius.

Fret Guard, plastic or cardboard guard shaped like a fretboard used to prevent the strings from damaging the frets during transport.

Fret Level, bar or flat plane used to grind the frets to an equal height.

Fret Tang, barbed stem under the fret used to hold the fret into a fretboard.

Fretwork, the forging, shaping and polishing of frets. Includes leveling, recrowning, installing and burnishing.

Fretboard, slab of material, usually wood, that contains frets.

Fretting Hammer, a specially designed hammer for installing frets.

Fulcrum, pivot point or support on which a lever turns in raising or moving something. Bridge that can be rocked forward and backward with a lever.

Ground, common reference point of contact in an electrical circuit.

Guitar Tuner, pitch or electronic reference device used to tune a guitar.

Hardtail, non-moving, non-fulcrum bridge.

Harmonic, generated tone whose rate of vibration is a precise multiple of that of a given fundamental tone.

Headstock, end of a neck containing the tuning keys and nut where the strings terminate.

Hemostats, clamping instrument used to hold one or more objects.

Hex Key, tool shaped as a hexagon used to adjust various components on a guitar.

Humbucker®, double-coiled, hum-cancelling magnetic pickup.

Humidifier, a device or machine that replaces moisture in an object or room.

Humidity, the amount of moisture in the air.

Hygrometer, gauge used to measure humidity.

Inertia Block, metal block that secures the counter balancing springs found in most fulcrum or tremolo style bridges.

Intonation, in unison, two notes matching in harmonic and fundamental pitch, adjustments to the nut and saddle that produce accurate pitches.

Leads, wires used to configure a pickup.

Leveling Bar, metal bar used to level, or grind frets.

Lever Switch, selector switch with a lever/cam mechanism.

LFT/W, left-wound coil, or wound for a left-handed or routed guitar.

Locking String Nut, metal string nut that locks the strings into place.

Lug, post or wiper where a wire is attached.

Luthier, one who builds and repairs stringed instruments.

Luthiers Guild, group of luthiers that meet for the exchange of information and advancement of the craft. Secret society of guitar builders plotting to rid the world of the banjo.

Magnet, ferrous (containing iron) material that can be magnetically charged to attract other ferrous materials. Each magnet has two ends, north end and south end. Each end (or pole) determines the direction of the current.

Magnetic, having the properties of a magnet.

Magnifying Lamp, lamp containing a magnifying lens.

Maintenance, care, upkeep and support.

Micrometer, an instrument for measuring very small distances extremely accurately.

Microphone, an instrument for intensifying weak signals by transforming sound waves electromagnetically into variations of electrical current.

Microphonic, having the properties of a microphone, prone to feedback.

Miniature Needle File, single-cut, carbide miniature file used for various repair projects on a guitar.

Neck Angle, the degree of angle the neck has in relationship to the bridge and top of a guitar.

Nut File, carbide, double-edged files available in various widths for cutting string slots into a nut.

Output Jack, electronic terminal that connects a guitar's electronics to an amplifier.

Parabolic Reflector, a spherical apparatus designed to focus, amplify, and direct sound.

Parallel, two circuits connected with both positives together and both negatives together so that the direction of the current is traveling in the same direction. This configuration will not hum-cancel.

Partial Refret, replacing some, but not all of the frets.

Passive Electronics, electrical circuit or circuits that do not require a power source (battery) in order to function.

Perpendicular, at right angles to a given plane or line.

Phase, the direction of current passing through one coil in relationship to a second coil.

Pickup, electronic coil that converts sound into an electromagnetic signal.

Pickup Balancing, equalizing the volume of a pickup in relationship to the strings and other pickups.

Piezo, a crystal that transmits an electrical signal when under pressure.

Precision Scale, 6" metal ruler used to measure in very small increments.

Primary, beginning or starting conductor in a circuit, pickup or harness.

Radius, the circular area or distance limited by the sweep of such line. The circular arch of a fretboard, bridge saddle or string nut.

Recrowning, to re-shape or reform the top and sides of a fret to its original shape.

Recrowning File, specially designed concave, half-round file for re-shaping frets.

Refret, total replacement of frets.

Relief, the degree of forebow or backbow in a neck.

Resonator, a guitar like instrument that utilizes a cone to generate an increase in resonance.

Rule of 18, equation that determines string nut and fret placement. Scale/17.817 = distance from the nut to the first fret.

RW/RP, reverse-wound/reverse polarity. Coil wound in reverse with reverse polarity to be hum-canceling when used with a traditional pickup coil.

Scuffmarks, scratches left in the top of a fret during the process of leveling.

Series, two circuits connected with the positive of one coil wired to the negative of the other so that the two coils hum-cancel.

Series Link, the lead(s) that connect two coils together in series.

Set-in Neck, glued-in, not a bolt-on neck.

Sharp, above the desired pitch, opposite of flat.

Signal, electrical impulse.

Single-Coil, pickup with only one coil.

Solder, tin/lead/rosin composite used to connect electrical components together.

Soldering Iron, electric iron that produces heat to melt solder.

Spring Claw, metal plate with hooks to hold tremolo springs to the inertia block.

SPST, single-pole/single-throw switch. Contains one row of three lugs consisting of one output and two inputs.

Start, beginning of a pickup coil or circuit.

Straightedges, metal stock milled extremely flat, used to gauge the forebow or backbow in a neck.

String Angle, the angle of a string in relationship to its beginning and termination points.

String Ferrells, metal tubular inserts that hold the ball end of a string in place on an electric guitar.

String Nut, bridge-like, slotted object that holds the strings in place at the headstock.

String Slots, channels cut at various depths and widths in the string nut.

String Spacing, the distance between each string slot.

String Tree, a disc, bar or T-shaped object that increases the angle of the string at the headstock.

String Winder, a device used to rapidly spin a tuning key button in order to speed up the process of re-stringing a guitar.

Tailpiece, apparatus that secures the strings of a guitar between the bridge and the tailblock.

Temperament, varying degrees of tuning each string of an instrument to produce a more pleasant sound when multiple strings are played at the same time.

Toggle Switch, two or three-way switch that is operated with a toggle.

Tone Potentiometer, electronic device that alters the tonality of a signal via attenuation.

Transducer, pickup that is activated by contact and vibration.

Transmit, force or energy, conveyed through a signal.

Tremolo Springs, counter-balancing springs that keep a tremolo bridge level.

Tremolo System, bridge system that works on a fulcrum or pivot points.

Trussrod, metal rod inside the neck of a guitar used to stabilize it.

Trussrod Nut, used to adjust the relief in a neck.

Tunematic®, fixed bridge with individual saddles and thumbwheels.

Tuning Key, mechanical device used to tighten or loosen guitar strings.

Variable, something that is likely to change.

Velocity, swiftness or speed of motion.

Volume Potentiometer, electronic device that alters volume of a signal via attenuation.

Wax Potting, the process of sealing a coil with wax to prevent microphonic feedback.

Wood Glue, water-based resin.

X-Acto® Knife, small sharp knife with a pencil-like handle.

X-Bridge®, electric guitar bridge with built-in piezo saddles.